MW00487728

That Woman

THE MAKING OF A TEXAS FEMINIST

WOMEN IN TEXAS HISTORY
Sponsored by the Ruthe Winegarten Memorial Foundation
Nancy Baker Jones and Cynthia J. Beeman, Series Editors

THAT WOMAN

The Making of a Texas Feminist

Nikki R. Van Hightower

Foreword by Nancy Baker Jones and Cynthia J. Beeman

Texas A&M University Press | College Station

This paper meets the requirements
of ANSI/NISO Z39.48–1992 (Permanence of Paper).
Binding materials have been chosen for durability.
Manufactured in the United States of America

Library of Congress Cataloging-in-Publication Data

Names: Hightower, Nikki Van, 1939– author.

Title: That woman: the making of a Texas feminist / Nikki R. Van Hightower;
  foreword by Nancy Baker Jones and Cynthia J. Beeman.

Other titles: Women in Texas history series.

Description: First edition. | College Station: Texas A&M University Press,
  [2020] | Series: Women in Texas history series | Includes bibliographical
  references and index. |

Identifiers: LCCN 2019046665 (print) | LCCN 2019046666 (ebook) | ISBN
  9781623498818 (ebook) | ISBN 9781623498801 (cloth) | ISBN
  9781623498801(cloth) | ISBN 9781623498818(ebook)

Subjects: LCSH: Hightower, Nikki Van, 1939– |
  Feminists—Texas—Houston—Biography. | Women
  politicians—Texas—Houston—Biography. |
  Politicians—Texas—Houston—Biography. | Houston (Tex.)—Politics and
  government—20th century. | LCGFT: Autobiographies.

Classification: LCC F394.H853 (ebook) | LCC F394.H853 H54 2020 (print) | DDC
  305.42092 [B]—dc23

LC record available at https://urldefense.proofpoint.com/v2/url?u=https-
3A__lccn.loc.gov_2019046665&d=DwIFAg&c=u6LDEWzohnDQ01ySGnxM
zg&r=bv66tK_oz9jwmvODs0ZjBQaLgA74Xy5S1julyhm3qOg&m=QDcHvV
5DU3QEF-BL_ygH3QKmYUGojkWtk7EVb2FNRhA&s=mZUy6R1EXJ5Up
chbO_RfYaksrc-pwK1hTUDXm9Fnwxc&e=

To the many volunteers and staff members
of the Houston Area Women's Center,
who have devoted enormous amounts
of time and energy over the years
to helping women in crisis

Contents

Foreword

In writing her memoir, Nikki Van Hightower professed to us that she intended "to examine the relationship between the small setting of my early life and the outside influences that opened my eyes to a much wider vision of the world." While this may be the most significant process an individual can undergo, achieving such awareness is not a given. Fortunately, Van Hightower has accomplished her goal, describing her transition from a child in a dysfunctional family into a respected and experienced Texas public servant and feminist who encountered some of the key figures of her time.

Van Hightower's story is appealing because it traces her self-propelled emergence from a childhood without mentors, with little emotional, educational, or financial support, and that was limited by gendered boundaries, into an intellectually curious, socially conscious, and politically aware adulthood that sought to change women's lives in a major American city—Houston. What she encountered on that journey was a newly energized feminist movement that challenged her to examine and reassess her sense of self. As with so many women who came of age in the mid-twentieth century without access to wealth, status, or the networks that came with them, Van Hightower *noticed* the creative disruption of the feminist movement's appearance and immediately made common cause with it. Feminism is the key ingredient in Van Hightower's metamorphosis.

In addition, she was moved, as she says, by the #MeToo movement in the twenty-first century, "a hideous reminder that women still endure brutal treatment and a clarion call to feminists: keep the women's movement alive, drive it further toward change, and address the mistreatments that still linger . . . , limiting women's rights as full human beings."

Her story takes readers through various employment and political campaigns, earning a PhD in political science, the sexism she experienced, the choices she made because of assumptions about women's "place" in personal and professional relationships, and the successes and losses she experienced, adding greatly to our understanding of the lives of professional women in the second half of twentieth-century Texas. As such, this memoir takes its place in the Women in Texas History book series sponsored by the Ruthe Winegarten Memorial Foundation for Texas Women's History.

Nancy Baker Jones and Cynthia J. Beeman
Series Editors

Preface

Had I not been relentlessly pressured to write this book by a very good friend I greatly respect, I probably never would have taken it on. She persuaded me that I have had worthwhile experiences from which others could benefit. She also convinced me that my life coincided with an important period for women that should be documented through the eyes of one who not only lived through it but was also deeply immersed in the gigantic efforts whereby women made substantial inroads in gaining equal rights with men. A new development in the women's movement also inspired me to write—the #MeToo movement was a hideous reminder that women still endure brutal treatment and a clarion call to feminists: keep the women's movement alive, drive it further toward change, and address the mistreatments that still linger—such as equal pay, sexual violence, health care, and racial justice—limiting women's rights as full human beings.

I was born in 1939, two years before the United States entered World War II, and my portion of the story concluded when I began writing in 2018, almost eight decades later. Being a feminist is hard work. The term itself implies a movement for change in the relationship between women and men. It means that we have to acknowledge each other as equals, support each other as equals, and communicate with each other as equals.

I was not born a feminist. I had not heard the expression until around 1969 when I entered graduate school at New York University to earn a PhD in political science. But the groundwork had been laid before then.

In chapter one, I relate an experience that opened my eyes to the intense resistance to women's rights by men who held power: My salary was reduced to $1 a year for taking my job as an advocate for women seriously. I learned that politics could be brutal, and that surviving the fray required belief in yourself and the legitimacy of your cause. In this chapter, I also reflect on the women's rights movement and what I believed was required of women to gain equal rights with men.

Starting in chapter two, I share some of my early experiences that took me down the path to feminist thinking, and I put my life into social and historical context. I passed through my teenage years in the 1950s—the glorious 1950s—when radio, television, and movies told us that real families were made up of white dads, who did important white-collar work and came home early enough to spend time with their families, and neatly dressed and attractive women, who were content in their domestic lives, and everyone was loyal and supportive of each other. My family was very unlike that image, and that made me sad. My sister and I went to a lot of movies, where the men were always in charge. When the men were good guys, the women were thrilled to be cared for; when the guys were bad, the women were glad to be rescued by good guys. Male dominance was the price of being rescued. Male dominance was the one constant that was reflected in our household, but it seemed quite different in the lives of the people on radio and in film.

Chapter three covers the powerful influence that education had on my life. With few exceptions, the world started to open up for me when I entered the university, particularly in graduate school, although there were still some strong similarities to my earlier life. The university faculty was dominated by men. Some felt comfortable openly supporting gender bias and sexually exploiting women students. I didn't consider doing anything about it then, but because of the occasional courage of other students I began to recognize that something could be done.

It was when I arrived at the dissertation stage of my PhD that my eyes really began to open. To gather data for my dissertation, entitled "The Politics of Female Socialization," I interviewed the women who ran for state and national office in the 1972 elections in New York City and Long Island. Four of the five women who won their elections considered themselves feminists. It became clear to me from their descriptions of the process of running that it was useful to have that mindset. This was a tough business. It required a firm sense of legitimacy to seek such leadership positions. These women had to be very strong, regarding themselves as equal to men—no one was going to rescue them or give them anything. Although I was not thinking of running for office at the time, it was clear to me that if I did so I would have to adopt their way of thinking.

Chapter four tells about my experience in a position I held in Houston city government called the Women's Advocate. This was my first real experience with politics. I took that title very seriously. There were no women elected city officials, nor had there ever been. The advocate was the only one charged to speak up for women's rights. As part of my hands-on political education, I learned that being an advocate in a political institution could be highly risky. You could be regarded as someone with split loyalties. I did not know that at the time, but it probably wouldn't have mattered. By that time, I was thinking like a feminist, and I was on the road fighting for equal rights for women, regardless of the costs.

One of the most remarkable experiences of my life was being a part of the 1977 International Women's Year National Conference, which was held in Houston. Chapter five tells of the IWY Conference and the energy and determination it infused into the women's rights movement. I was fortunate to be an active part of the planning and one of the conference representatives from Texas. The Houston conference made us address our own misunderstandings of each other in terms of race, religion, ethnicity, social class, and sexual orientation. It effectively forced us out of our comfort zones, making the movement much stronger and more diverse as a result.

In chapter six, "A Short Media Career," I relate my experience of the power of the media—radio in this case. I received a hands-on lesson in how those in political power make every effort to manage the information that goes out to the public. It was a mixed experience for me, because what made me attractive to the media (my activism and the resulting controversy) made me threatening to those in power. I was used by the media, but I took advantage of the opportunity to use them.

As I describe in chapter seven, my very rocky path ultimately led me to the outcome I had been working toward for several years. I finally had the chance to achieve my goal of truly being a women's advocate, and this time I was leading a whole group of feminist advocates. By opening the Houston Area Women's Center, we served the needs of women and children who were in crisis because of the abuse that results from the disproportionate power of men over women. The Houston Area Women's Center provided a nonjudgmental, feminist environment where dedicated people helped guide them toward whatever they wanted for their lives.

Chapter eight tells of my experiences as a candidate for elective office. Ever since my time in city government, I had longed to serve as an elected official. In those early years of women seeking office, my desire to serve overcame any anxiety I felt. As a neophyte, I had a lot to learn. I was a candidate for office three times, or if you count runoffs and primaries, I actually was a candidate seven times. I lost two times and won once in the general elections. I gained a significant amount of experience in both situations. Losing was painful. Winning was a trip. But, as I explain in this chapter, there is much more to being in public office than winning.

Candidacy is a real test of stamina in every way: physical, psychological, financial, and emotional. I had other painful and public losses leading up to my campaign. I have often been told, "You must really have a thick skin." I am not sure I know what a thick skin is. I don't think I have it. In retrospect, what I did have was determination when I really wanted something. It wasn't that failure to achieve what I wanted didn't hurt. It did. I licked my wounds for a while, sometimes longer than other times, but as soon as I felt a little healing, I started making new plans. It was very important to have friends and advisors around me for support and courage and to help me keep losses in perspective.

One misunderstanding I had about elective office was that I would have a great deal more power than I had as a nongovernmental activist. In retrospect, I overestimated the power of elected officials and I underestimated the power of activists. The latter is particularly true if you are good at organizing, which I believe I was. If you can get a lot of people working toward a goal, it can be quite threatening to elected officials.

The last chapter of the book, chapter nine, winds up my career. I returned to teaching, this time at Texas A&M University in College

Station, Texas. For the first time in my life, I actually enjoyed teaching. In my earlier teaching positions, I had always struggled with feeling unsure about my level of knowledge. After about fifteen years of fighting battles in politics, confidence in the subject was no longer an issue. I knew what I was talking about and I had lots of stories to tell. Much of the increase in confidence was the result of experience, but it also came from my greater understanding of the context of that experience. As a woman, I had acquired certain ways of thinking growing up, about my abilities and my place in the world. My work in the feminist movement showed me a path out of those self-limitations. It took a long time, and I still have not completely overcome that early socialization, but I now recognize the effects of brainwashing when it appears, something I could not have imagined without the tremendous influence of the women's rights movement and feminism.

Acknowledgments

Until I started work on this memoir, I thought of writing as a lonely endeavor. Yet as I prepared notes for my acknowledgments, I realized that I was far from alone. I wrote with the memories, encouragement, and guidance of a staggering number of people who have moved through my life for more years than I can remember. How fortunate I am.

I must begin my acknowledgments by thanking the one person most responsible for the genesis and development of this book project. She has requested that she remain anonymous, and so I will honor that request however much I wish to share my appreciation of her with the world. Nonetheless, I am compelled to document here how inspired I was and am by her relentless insistence that I had a meaningful story to tell. That insistence sprang from her belief that people, particularly young women, would benefit if I shared my experiences. She read and reread every page and provided much needed moral support throughout the entire process. I thank you, —, so very much.

Some of the people who guided me in the difficult early days include Dr. David Woodcock, professor emeritus of architecture at Texas A&M University and a wonderful neighbor, and Dr. Elizabeth Gregory, director of women's, gender, and sexuality studies and professor of English at the University of Houston. An institution that played a key role in providing me with valuable materials is the Carey C. Shuart Women's Research Collection at the University of Houston Libraries. I donated all of my papers to this collection at the University of Houston library, and they have taken excellent care of them. I also want to thank Dr. Judith A. Baer, Professor Emerita of Political Science at Texas A&M University, who guided me through the early stages of the arduous path of publishing.

I relied on some of the closest friends in my life to read the first drafts of these chapters and provide me with their thoughts, which I knew would be brutally honest. I was not disappointed. Among these early readers was Dr. Susan MacManus, distinguished professor emerita in the School of Interdisciplinary Global Studies at the University of South Florida. Susan and I first met during the academic year of 1976–1977 when we were on the faculty at the University of Houston. She has published numerous books and articles. Included in this group is my sister, Sharylee Clark, who has carefully read every revision, and my life partner, Raul Castillo, who read, critiqued, and gave valuable suggestions. Susan and Raul had shared my years of activism, and Sharylee was invaluable in aiding my faulty memory of the early years of my life. Invaluable to this work were my editors at Texas A&M University Press, Dr. Shannon Davies, director, and Emily Seyl, acquisitions editor. They have been a joy to work with both because of their professional guidance and because they are delightful people. I have looked forward to every meeting I have had with them. I expected the process to be painful. It was anything but! I want to thank the Texas A&M Press, as an institution, for believing in the historical and political value of this memoir. I also want to give special thanks to Nancy Baker Jones and Cynthia J. Beeman, of the Ruthe Winegarten Memorial Foundation for Texas Women's History, for their decision to include my memoir in the Women in Texas History book series. I consider that inclusion a great honor.

Others who gave me much-welcomed support and encouragement include Dr. Marilyn Falik, a dear friend of mine from graduate school at New York University, and many friends and family members. Thousands of others shared the real-life experiences with me: members of the Mid-Suffolk (Long Island, New York) chapter of the National Organization for Women (NOW); the Huntington (Long Island, New York) chapter of NOW; the Houston chapter of NOW; former Houston mayor Fred Hofheinz; City of Houston women employees; volunteers and staff of the Houston Area Women's Center, who were always patient with my impatience; delegates to the International Women's Year at the Texas state conference in Austin, TX, and to the national conference in Houston; my students at Texas A&M University; and, finally, Poppy Northcutt, who set a wonderful example of how brave a woman can be.

That Woman

THE MAKING OF A TEXAS FEMINIST

1 A Dollar a Year

In May 1976, I landed what was for me the perfect job: I was appointed to the position of Women's Advocate for the City of Houston by Mayor Fred Hofheinz. It was the only such position in the country.

Ten months later, I was attending an afternoon meeting at city hall when, to the surprise of all of us, a group of media representatives walked in loaded with cameras and notepads. With eyes focused on me and cameras rolling, someone asked if I were aware that the members of the city council had just reduced my salary from $18,000 to $1 per year. Tension filled the room as everyone waited for my response. Baffled, I asked them to repeat what they had just said. It wasn't that I hadn't heard them; I didn't understand what was happening and needed an extra minute to pull my thoughts together. Something vague spilled out of my mouth like, "Well, this is news to me, I'd better see what's going on." I stood up, excused myself, and headed to the mayor's office.

The mayor was also in a meeting, so I planted myself in his waiting room, intending to stay there as long as it took to talk to him. What I had just learned was seriously disturbing. I had been involved in the women's rights movement for several years, beginning in 1972 as a member of the National Organization for Women (NOW) in Long Island, New York. I had a passionate commitment to feminism, and, after being lucky enough to find a position where I believed I could really make a difference, it seemed now to be slipping away. I wasn't sure if I had any support or if I would simply be ushered out with my final paycheck of $1.

I knew what the reduction to $1 per year meant. In a dramatic move, the council members were expressing what they thought not only of my role as the Women's Advocate but also of the women's rights movement as a whole. When I had accepted the position, one of the all-male city council members had been quoted in the *Houston Chronicle* as saying that "the Advocate was not necessary . . . a waste of taxpayers' money." The complainer was probably thinking of city taxes, though funding for the office of Women's Advocate came from the federal government.

What I felt as I sat there waiting for the mayor was not merely anxiety from the loss of a salary and, presumably, a job that I cared deeply about, as well as the resulting humiliation. It was more than that. No woman had ever been elected to any office in Houston's city government, and the Women's Advocate position had been created by the mayor in response to pressure by activists who wanted better representation for women's needs. I took that very seriously. Long before I knew anything about feminism or the feminist movement, I recognized that women were shortchanged in multiple ways, and I had built up a lot of anger over the years of being a woman in this male-dominated society. Until I became part of the women's rights movement, I didn't think there was anything that could be done about it. Now I was wondering if I had been correct in my earlier assessment.

After what felt like forever, the mayor finally returned. He didn't seem surprised to see me. After the miserably long wait, I was immediately put at ease by his explanation of the situation. Supposedly, the council was reacting to a keynote speech I had given at a rally in support of the passage of the Equal Rights Amendment and a woman's right to have an abortion. The week following the rally, several citizens complained that it was inappropriate for me to take a public position in support of those issues. The council immediately decided to reduce my salary to $1 per year. The mayor vehemently opposed the move.

He assured me that he supported me in the job I was doing. The elected city controller, Leonel Castillo, who had been ordered by the city council to make the change in my salary, refused to do so. Furthermore, the city's legal department had issued a statement informing the council that they did not have the authority to make any changes in my salary. Mayor Hofheinz encouraged me to carry on the work I was doing, reassuring me that my salary would not be reduced.

Houston
Breakthrough
Where Women Are News

Vol. II, No. 4   April 1977   50 cents

SPECIAL ISSUE: THE WOMEN'S ADVOCATE
DR. NIKKI VAN HIGHTOWER

A disappointing moment following the Houston City Council's vote to reduce the Women's Advocate's salary to $1 per year. Courtesy of Houston Breakthrough *magazine.*

Media coverage of this confrontation quickly spread throughout the country. The coverage was generally of a humorous nature with the brunt of it targeted at the city council members. What happened to me that day in Houston was but one in a very long list of injustices to women, but it served as a reminder of the struggles of the many women who came before me.

For women, the early history of this country was one of second-class citizenship. Largely restricted to home and family, women were denied property rights, the right to keep any wages they earned, to sign contracts, and, of course, the right to vote. The earliest efforts for change addressed a broad spectrum of issues, such as the ones just mentioned.

In 1848, the first real convention for women's rights, organized by Lucretia Mott and Elizabeth Cady Stanton, was held at Seneca Falls, New York. More than 250 women and about forty men attended. At the time of Seneca Falls, women were not mentioned in the US Constitution. At the convention, women claimed the right to vote and own property, and demanded that they be given opportunities for better education and other personal and public rights. It has often been said by those who study women's history that marriage for women at the time was comparable to "civil death." When a woman married, all rights and property shifted to her husband. The dominant thinking was that when a couple married, they became one. For all intents and purposes, that one was the husband.

The Seneca Falls Convention concluded with sixty-eight women and thirty-two men signing a Declaration of Sentiments, patterned after the US Declaration of Independence:

> We hold these truths to be self-evident, that all men and women are created equal, that they are endowed by their creator with certain inalienable rights, that among these are life, liberty, and the pursuit of happiness; that to secure these rights governments are instituted, deriving their just powers from the consent of the governed.

As it turned out, the convention became known primarily for the demand for suffrage, and, ironically, the most conflict was generated by the resolution for suffrage rights.

Following the Civil War, in 1868 and 1870 respectively, the

Fourteenth and Fifteenth Amendments to the Constitution were ratified, giving civil rights (Fourteenth) and the right to vote (Fifteenth) to all male citizens. Women had hoped to be included in this broad extension of rights but were instead explicitly excluded by the use of the word "male" in the Fourteenth Amendment—the first time the Constitution had specifically referred to gender. It was a crushing setback for the women's movement activists and women in general.

Seventy-two years after the 1848 Seneca Falls Convention—seventy-two years of intense struggle and sacrifice on the part of the suffragists—the Nineteenth Amendment giving women the right to vote was ratified. It was a long and exhausting battle, and even though they won the right to vote, women continued to be denied full protection under the Constitution.

One of the significant leaders of the women's suffrage movement, Carrie Chapman Catt, warned at the 1920 victory convention of the National Woman Suffrage Association (NWSA), "If you stay there long enough and are active enough, you will see something else—the real thing in the center, with the door locked tight, and you will have a long hard fight before you get behind that door, for there is the engine that moves the wheels of your party machinery. Nevertheless, it will be an interesting and thrilling struggle and well worthwhile. If you really want women's vote to count, make your way there."

While serving as president of the NWSA and following up on her concern of post-suffrage activism, Catt founded the League of Women Voters in 1920. Her belief was that the league would educate women about voting and politics and thereby transform American political life for the good.

Regretfully, Catt's utopian vision of women's suffrage seemed to apply only to white women. Catt, along with other white suffragists, left a stain on the movement by using racism to appeal to Southern states to ratify the Nineteenth Amendment. She is noted in the New York Times archives for a well-known quote: "White supremacy will be strengthened, not weakened by women's suffrage."

In the 1960s, about forty years after the passage of the Nineteenth Amendment, new generations of women once again began to organize. Over the course of those years, women had become better educated; they had entered the workforce in large numbers, especially during and after World War II; and they had continued to engage in public life. Taking aim at a wide range of issues, the movement focused on equal employment and educational opportunities, family relationships, reproductive rights including abortion, credit rights, and violence against women.

Key books that helped shape and inspire the movement included Simone de Beauvoir's 1949 *The Second Sex* and Betty Friedan's 1963 *The Feminine Mystique*. Under pressure from women's groups, President Kennedy established the Presidential Commission on the Status of Women, chaired by Eleanor Roosevelt. Other major influences on the movement included development of the oral contraceptive pill, which helped women control their reproductivity, and the formation of a powerful organization, the National Organization for Women, in 1966.

Many women were introduced to the movement by "consciousness-raising," a concept described by Anne Forer Pyne in the mid-1970s. Small groups of women would get together and share their personal experiences of discrimination, injustice, and unfairness. "As women shared their firsthand accounts of slights and injustices they had endured—at work, at home and in the bedroom—they found patterns, and solidarity. Experiences that they assumed had been theirs alone turned out to be collective, and swapping stories became one of the foundational tools of the Second Wave feminist movement."

In 1972, the Equal Rights Amendment (ERA), which was first introduced in 1923 by famed suffragist Alice Paul, was finally passed by the US Congress. The twenty-four plain words of the Equal Rights Amendment are as follows:

Section 1. Equality of rights under the law shall not be denied or abridged by the United States or by any state on account of sex.
Section 2. The Congress shall have the power to enforce, by appropriate legislation, the provisions of the article.
Section 3. This Amendment shall take effect two years after ratification.

Amending the US Constitution requires a two-thirds vote in both houses of Congress, followed by ratification of three-fourths (or thirty-eight) of the state legislatures. The state ratification process won the support of only thirty-five states, falling three votes short. The amendment would have made women explicitly equal under the Constitution, with the word "women" inserted for the first time. Not having it there leaves little constitutional protection when either states or the federal government choose to ignore the rights of women. Many of the worst violations to women's rights have been corrected by an array of federal legislation, but when I was the Women's Advocate in Houston in the 1970s, many loopholes in the laws protecting women's rights remained, particularly in state laws.

Supreme Court Justice Ruth Bader Ginsburg made the following statement about her support of the Equal Rights Amendment at a 2014 talk at the National Press Club:

> If I could choose an Amendment to add to the Constitution, it would be the Equal Rights Amendment . . . I think we have achieved that through legislation, but legislation can be repealed, it can be altered. So I would like my granddaughters, when they pick up the Constitution, to see that notion—that women and men are persons of equal stature—I'd like them to see that this is the basic principle of our society.

Since the deadline for ratification was 1982, it was assumed that the Equal Rights Amendment was dead. Surprisingly, there are still signs of life. Nevada approved the amendment in 2017 and Illinois in 2018. Great hope was put on Virginia, where polls show there is overwhelming support among voters, to be the thirty-eighth state to ratify, but the ratification measure died by one vote in a committee in the House of Delegates. The house tried to force it out of committee, but the vote was 50–50, and to do so would have required fifty-one votes. As Garrett Epps reported in the *Atlantic*, even if it had passed, finally providing the necessary thirty-eight states for ratification, passage would still have to overcome numerous anticipated court battles over the matter of the 1982 ratification deadline and also the legitimacy of four states rescinding their ratifications. The legal battle will be a tough one. As they say, "Where there is life, there is hope."

2 Family

I was born in Billings, Montana, in 1939, two years before the attack on Pearl Harbor in 1941 instantly catapulted the United States into World War II. Billings was the third largest city in the state. We later moved to a cold, grim little town called Chinook for a few years, then to Cut Bank, a small town just south of the Canadian border—also cold with miserable winters—where I started school. We relocated back to Billings when I was in the sixth grade. Like all children, the first years of life established in me a sense of what was normal, whether it was or not. For me, normal was growing up in Montana, and I believed that Montana, with its mountains and prairies, was the way the world looked. Normal for me was also being raised by my grandmother while calling her "Mother"—thinking of her as my mother but realizing there was another mother out there somewhere who had a connection to me. Normal was living with a harsh, domineering, and sometimes abusive grandfather. Normal was having three older brothers (my grandparents' children) who were not brothers at all. The oldest and youngest were uncles and the middle one was my biological father, whom I adored but never really thought of as a father. What I thought was normal while growing up I later learned was definitely not.

My sister, Sharylee, was sixteen months older than I, and together we sorted out normal from abnormal as we grew up. My biological mother, Lois, was fifteen years old when she became pregnant with Sharylee. Lois and her family were nearby neighbors to our family in Billings. She was friends with and went to school with my grandparents' two older sons, Quentin and "Bud." The relationship with Bud moved beyond friendship. Not much was said about

*Nikki (right), age two, playing with a toy snake, and sister Sharylee (left).
At home in Chinook, Montana.*

*Nikki circa age six with
pet cat in Cut Bank,
Montana.*

Lois in our family, but when the subject of her and her family did come up, there was a clear sense of bitterness and contempt.

My grandmother was the one most willing to talk about our family history, and, although she expressed sadness for Lois and Bud, it was clear she believed that the blame for the pregnancy lay with Lois and Lois's mother. The understanding my sister and I held was that Lois's mother had encouraged her to "get" one of the boys. The supposed motivation for this was that our family was economically and socially superior to her family, and Lois's mother saw an opportunity for her daughter to take a step up the ladder. Clearly my grandmother was aggrieved for her son, whose life was changed so drastically at such an early age in the midst of the Great Depression. He was seventeen years old. The lesson for my sister and me was that boys were not to be trusted when it came to sex, and that it was the responsibility of "good" girls to be careful and manage the situation. Mothers had the ultimate responsibility for keeping their girls "good."

Thus, in the eyes of our family, Lois's mother harbored most of the blame for the unwanted pregnancy, although my grandmother did not consider herself free of guilt by any means. She was out of town when it happened, on a trip to visit her sister in Oregon, leaving her two teenage sons alone with their father for a few weeks. To the best of my knowledge, our grandfather seemed to escape the burden of any guilt. He had his own responsibilities earning a living for the family in the oil transportation business. He wasn't responsible for domestic affairs. They were the responsibility of our grandmother. It was clear that he had little understanding of or interest in the lives of the females in the family.

The unwanted pregnancy forced the teenagers, Bud and Lois, into marriage. Sharylee and I lived with them, our biological parents, when we were infants; however, I have no memories of that time. The young couple divorced within about three years. My grandmother and biological father, Bud, were given joint custody of my sister and me. All I learned regarding the divorce was what my grandmother told me. Her explanation for why Lois lost full parental rights was that she misbehaved in court, which had something to do with mouthing off to the judge, who was—as all were at the time—a man. The exact circumstances were never explained. After the divorce, Lois dropped out of the picture as far as my sister and I were concerned. We were told that she remarried and moved to California. Her parents (our other grandparents) remained in Billings, and occasionally we saw them when we were able to keep it a secret from our grandfather. He never held back his hatred of them.

After the divorce, we called our grandmother "Mother," our grandfather "Grandpa," and Bud, our biological father, "Daddy Bud." Exactly why or how these names were selected I do not recall, but they remained so for many years.

The secrets of our family were not kept from my sister and me, but neither were they openly discussed. We were told not to share them with anyone outside the family. We followed these rules, partly because we sensed that there was a shamefulness about our family and that the shame was most likely linked to our births.

Although my biological father, Bud, shared custody of Sharylee and me, for all practical purposes he took little interest in or responsibility for our lives. During World War II, he served in the merchant marines from 1942 until 1946. It was dangerous duty carrying supplies to those in combat in the Pacific. We were thrilled when the war ended and he came home, which at that time was in Cut Bank, Montana. I thought I would be able to spend time with him and really get to know him. He was handsome and funny, and we adored him. As it turned out, my hopes were pretty much shattered. He was home from the war, but not much changed. We

Biological father, "Bud," in World War II merchant marine uniform. At home in Cut Bank, Montana.

still saw very little of him. My grandmother usually made excuses for his absences, explaining that he had work demands that often took him out of town, and that he wished he could be with us, but his work kept him away. Her one criticism of him was that he never paid any child support, which troubled her. It was my impression that she suspected he was making up for the good times he missed after the unplanned pregnancy and during the war.

Approximately 350,000 women served in the US Armed Forces at home and abroad during World War II. They served as Women Airforce Service Pilots (WASPS) and in roles in the Army, Navy, Coast Guard, and Marine Corps. Only recently have the Women Airforce Service Pilots been recognized for their bravery and essential contribution to the war effort. On the home front, women took up the slack in the industrial labor force, filling in for men who were in the military. The iconic image of Rosie the Riveter was used as propaganda to attract women into the factories that were manufacturing industrial materials for the war, jobs that had until then been closed to women.

Regardless of the crucial roles women played in the war, the public learned little about them. Working women were largely absent from the World War II movies I watched as I grew up. Those movies were about the bravery and sacrifice of men. We learned that men fought the war and women and children waited for their return. A woman's sacrifice was depicted mainly as widowhood.

When Bud and his older brother, Quentin, entered the war, I was keenly aware that my grandmother was terribly worried about the safety of her sons, and their letters came from places largely unknown to all of us. I knew we paid for groceries with coupons, and kids could no longer buy bubble gum. What I did not learn about at the time was any significant contribution that women were making to the war effort.

Three years after the war ended, Bud remarried, settled down in Cut Bank, established his own commercial paint company, and started a new family. Just prior to his wedding ceremony, which Sharylee and I attended, Bud called us aside and requested that we drop the "Daddy" in "Daddy Bud" and just call him "Bud." It must have hurt us, but, surprisingly, neither my sister nor I can recall much about our feelings that day. Bud was caught up in his new life, and to our dismay we learned somewhat later that his new wife, who was also named Lois, was not thrilled about having us around. This was another reason for him to distance himself from my sister and me. I envied his new children, of whom he seemed to be very fond.

When I was about thirteen years old, I began to recognize that Bud had a dark side. His humor was mainly based on sarcasm, which I found hilarious when the target was someone else, but the meanness of it was also turned on me and my sister, particularly as we reached puberty. As an example, after we had moved with my grandparents back to Billings, on rare occasions Sharylee and I visited Bud and his family in Cut Bank. On one of those visits, he and I were sitting at his kitchen table when Sharylee came in the room. She was unusually nicely dressed, probably to please Bud, but her dress was old and the hem uneven. He looked up when she entered, and his comment was, "My god, you look like hell." I laughed until I saw the pain on her face and the tears beginning to roll down her cheeks. She flew out of the room, and, as I recall, I ran after her, belatedly recognizing that the remark was not funny. During the same visit, he ridiculed the acne on my face and my weight, which was too heavy by his standards. The remarks hurt, but he laughed, so I also tried to laugh.

Sharylee and I learned much later that Bud and his second wife never told their children that Sharylee and I were their half-sisters. They said it was quite a shock when they finally learned about it. They were told that we were the children of our grandparents and they never questioned that.

To our surprise, when we were in junior high school, our grand-father requested that we call him "Dad." I do not doubt that the two men felt awkward about this, but the names "Dad" and "Daddy" didn't have a whole lot of meaning to my sister and me. From what we had learned from books, magazines, and experiences with other families, neither man really fit the part.

Around 1990, when Sharylee and I were both midlife adults, Lois, our biological mother, contacted us and requested that we plan to visit her and her latest husband in Santa Fe, New Mexico, where Sharylee and her husband lived at the time. I was married and lived in Houston, Texas, and was quite curious about the idea of meeting her for the first time, at least in my memory. I tried to weigh my feelings about the prospect, but curiosity was all I could come up with. I sensed no lingering emotions. As it turned out, it was a rather meaningless experience. Lois seemed uneasy talking about her earlier life and stayed very much a stranger to me. I have always been curious about what she wanted or expected from that visit in Santa Fe. Maybe it was curiosity on her part as well. There was no evidence that she yearned to get to know us. She kept her husband around at all times, and the conversation stayed at a very superficial level. We never saw her again, and she died about

First meeting since early childhood with biological mother, Lois (center), and Sharylee (right), circa 1988.

thirty years later. In her lifetime, she had four husbands and eight children, including me and my sister. I never met any of her other children. From the short time we spent with her, it was clear that she had a problem with alcohol. The meeting left me with a great sense of relief that it was my grandmother who had ended up with custody of my sister and me.

I learned several brutal lessons from my biological mother's early, unwanted pregnancies. First, women were the ones mostly at fault. Second, though I have no firm knowledge about the circumstances of our mother losing full custody of my sister and me, there was an unspoken lesson about smarting off to a male authority. Also, although I was not fully conscious of it, I know I carried negative feelings about my biological mother that never fully went away. The negativity on my part wasn't necessarily about the pregnancy but about not feeling any pride in her and the way she conducted her life afterward.

When I was in the sixth grade, my grandparents, my sister, and I moved back to Billings. I didn't know the reason for the move at the time but found out later that my grandmother had cervical cancer that had metastasized. Cut Bank lacked the medical facilities for the treatment she needed. The change must have been a great relief for Bud and his second wife. To some degree it was a relief for me as well, because it meant a new beginning and it was easier to maintain the cover-up of our odd family structure. I still missed Bud and longed for his companionship, but we rarely saw him after that.

Most of my memories of my grandfather are of an angry and unhappy man. His stepsister, the only woman he seemed to respect, told me that he'd had a difficult childhood, raised by a stepmother who had little use for him. I learned very little from him directly. What I did hear from him was that, compared to his children and grandchildren, he had been poorer, worked harder, and lived under more dire circumstances. In his mind, we had a very comfortable life and should be grateful for it. I had no doubt that was true, but I did not understand why that should be justification for his anger. We, after all, had no more choice about the quality of our lives than he did.

Our grandfather was an intelligent man with little education

—fourth grade, I was told. Much of his adult life he spent working in the oil fields or trucking oil products. He was not a person with business skills, and debt always seemed to follow quickly after any financial success. The cost of our grandmother's illness added to the financial stress, which also added to his anger.

He could be violent when he interpreted our words or behavior as lacking in proper respect or deference. He occasionally knocked me around and once choked and slammed me against the wall. There were many other threats, but usually they were not carried through. My grandmother told me of times when he had hit her with his fist. I once witnessed him kicking a box of talcum powder at her. The box landed on her foot. She was very ill with cancer at the time, and her foot was badly swollen the next day. Most of the time, he wasn't actually physically violent, he simply created an atmosphere of dread by slamming doors, stomping when he walked, and yelling instead of talking in a normal voice.

My grandmother told me that the two oldest sons had been the victims of the worst of his physical violence. That ended when they were old enough and big enough to fight back. Quentin left home when he finished high school and enlisted with the marines. My grandmother told me that my grandfather seemed to regard Bud differently after Lois's unplanned pregnancy, showing more respect and support during that time. I never figured out what that was about.

We were all aware that my grandfather had relationships with other women. I know it hurt my grandmother terribly. I, however, was baffled that any woman found him attractive and was just glad to have him out of the house.

My sister and I dreaded our grandfather's so-called affection almost as much as his anger. When we asked him for money to go to a movie, he would insist that we sit on his lap to make the request. He would then tease us obnoxiously by licking us on the face and sticking his tongue in our ears. We would force ourselves to giggle and plead, knowing we would eventually get what we wanted if we offered no resistance. If our grandmother was watching, she would say something like, "Oh, Dad," with a pained smile on her face. She knew we hated the fondling, but no one stood up to him. As soon as the misery was over, we would hurry to wash our faces and rush out.

I had little sense of what, if any, genuine feelings he had for my sister and me. As we neared high school graduation, he expressed no pride in our earning our diplomas. He seemed mostly concerned about us leaving the care of his very sick wife in his hands. It's true that I never heard him express any resentment about our living in the household, probably because on that issue our grandmother would have put up a real battle.

I held a deep affection for my grandmother, not that our relationship was always rosy. Sharylee and I had our sisterhood battles, which annoyed everyone. My grandmother followed the common discipline practices of her time, not sparing the rod when we were younger. Throughout her life she suffered serious health problems and relied heavily on my sister and me to help around the house and provide care for her as she became more incapacitated.

Sharylee and I were close to my grandmother, and, particularly when my sister and I were younger, we three entertained ourselves with board games, card games, radio programs, books, movies, and music. Our grandmother saw to it that we took piano lessons—we had lots of sheet music and often played and sang together. She loved us and was interested in our lives and, for the large part, understood them. But she also understood the dangers we were likely to put ourselves in. Our grandmother always liked our girlfriends and their families. She was less certain of some of the boys we dated, but in general she tolerated our choices. When Sharylee and I entered our teenage years, we became increasingly independent of her. Having been so closely involved in Bud and Lois's unwanted pregnancy, she clearly was deeply concerned the experience might repeat itself. But she never said anything to our grandfather when we became unruly for fear of the consequences.

On the whole, our grandfather did not take part in the domestic life of our household and had no interest in the situation being otherwise. His trucking business often kept him out on the road, which was a great relief to us. In Billings, he had a large shop right next to the house, so the times he was in town were stressful. Our grandmother kept close track of his whereabouts. I remember that when he was headed for the house during times we were not in school, she would call out, "Girls, girls, Dad's here—act like you're busy." I worked in a dime store one Christmas break, and found it

was a lot like my home: the other clerks would spread the word—
"Look like you're busy; the manager is here!"—so I would start
reshuffling the goods on the counters.

My grandmother was a high school graduate and stayed well
informed about the issues of the day. She was a devoted reader,
which she encouraged us to be as well. We would sometimes read
aloud, passing a book around so we all got a share of reading
time. When my sister and I had upcoming piano recitals, or acting
roles or speeches to perform at school, she insisted that we practice over and over again at home, where she would critique our
performances. That seemingly small effort on her part has taught
me the importance of preparation and played a major beneficial
role in my life. My abilities in public speaking link directly to her
encouragement and discipline during my early life.

Our accomplishments in school gave our grandmother a great
deal of pride. Unless she was too ill, she would attend the school
functions or performances in which we participated—just the
opposite of our grandfather. She created a picture of life for us
that was full of success. The problem was that other than her
encouragement, of which she freely gave, she had no actual way
of helping us: no money, no contacts, no means of transportation.
It was her youngest son, married and living in Tulsa, Oklahoma,
who encouraged Sharylee and me to attend the University of Tulsa,
where we both received partial scholarships. It might have made
more economic sense for us to attend a nearby college and live at
home, but our grandmother believed strongly that it was important we got far away from the dominance of our grandfather and
his limited thinking for our future. She was seriously ill during
our high school years but was determined to see us take our first
independent steps in life. She died of cancer during my first year
at the University of Tulsa.

Our grandmother was always willing to share information about
her early life growing up, and my sister and I both regret that we
didn't ask her more questions. She loved her family, who were first-
generation emigrants from Norway. She described them as gentle
and loving. Sadly, life with her family was short. Her mother died
in childbirth when she was around twelve or thirteen years old,
and her father died a few years later. My grandmother and her

younger siblings were placed in foster homes, a lonely and difficult experience. After an older sister married, she lived with her
in Minnesota, where she met her future husband.

After high school, my grandmother trained to be a telegrapher.
She told us stories about looking for a job and facing the difficulties of competing with men for employment. One such experience
happened after she completed telegraph school during a test to
determine the qualifications of the participants. She was the only
woman in the group. "All the men stared at me," she said. "I looked
down at my telegraph machine, but they kept staring and I was
nervous to begin with. Tears started to roll down my face and I was
so embarrassed that I just got up and left." I felt so angry for her and
at her. "Why didn't you just ignore them?" I demanded. "I couldn't,"
she said, and tears came to her eyes once again even after all those
years. She did eventually find a job as a telegrapher in a local hotel,
where she said people treated her well. Later in my life, I too felt
the anxiety of being the lone woman in a field of men.

One of my greatest regrets is not ever asking her feelings about
or experience with the suffrage movement. She was born in 1892
and would have been twenty-eight years old when the suffrage
amendment passed in 1920. She had considerable interest in
politics and never missed an opportunity to vote; I watched her
fill out her absentee ballot when she was near death. I would love
to have heard her thoughts on the suffrage movement or to know
if she were involved. When I think about her, I get angry at myself
for being so thoughtless about her experiences, though at the time
I was quite ignorant.

My grandmother was a committed Republican, and as a result
I grew up identifying as a Republican until I was in college. I can't
help but believe that she would have been supportive of the resur-
gence of the women's movement then, but, regardless, I give her
credit for preparing me to become a leader in the movement. I
strongly believe my grandmother, who experienced a great deal
of personal pain and humiliation for being a woman, would have
welcomed the modern feminist movement and its brave leaders.

After graduating from high school in Billings in 1957, I went to
college at the University of Tulsa. Even with a partial scholarship, I
was always painfully short of money, and I was lonely and homesick

High school senior photo.

for my friends in Billings. The University of Tulsa, like most universities at the time, set rigid curfews for female students (but none for the male students). I felt claustrophobic and out of touch, and my tendency toward rule-breaking kept me in trouble much of the time. After one unhappy year residing in the girls' dorm in Tulsa, I dropped out of college and went to work for Avis Rent-a-Car.

Another reason I was unhappy was that I didn't really have a reason for being there other than the fact that as a (soon to be) working girl of the middle class, going to college was what you did at that time in your life. Nothing at school particularly interested me. I was just putting in time.

I was more comfortable in the workforce. As ordinary jobs go, I liked the work at Avis Rent-a-Car. I particularly liked it when a new city manager was brought in. Irvin was nine years older than I and, from my perspective, knew his way around the world. It didn't hurt that he was very nice-looking and attracted to me. He had served in the air force in Korea and had done a considerable amount of traveling with his job at Avis. We started dating. After only a year in Tulsa, he was transferred to St. Louis, Missouri. We decided to get married and move to St. Louis together in 1960.

In 1967, after Irvin and I had moved from St. Louis to Houston, I made plans to attend my ten-year high school reunion in Billings. My high school friends and I had stayed in touch with each other, and I still had positive memories of my life there. As Sharylee had done the year before when she went to her reunion, I contacted Bud to see if he could meet me sometime during my trip. He and his family were still living in Cut Bank. He agreed, and I was delighted. It would be the first time in my life I would be with him as an adult, just he and I. We made plans to have dinner one evening, and he would leave the next morning.

Nikki and Irvin's wedding, July 9, 1960.

We had dinner in the hotel where he was staying, and for several hours afterward we talked and laughed and drank. I felt like I was finally getting to know Bud. He suggested that rather than getting out on the road after some pretty heavy drinking, we go to his room and get some sleep; he would take me back to my friend's house in the morning. He and Sharylee had done the same thing the year before, which she had told me about, and it seemed like a reasonable suggestion. We lay down on the bed with our clothes on, and I fell immediately asleep. Waking up the next morning, I realized he was sliding his hand down the waistband of my slacks, and it seemed evident that he was trying to molest me. I froze for a few seconds to determine if I were misinterpreting the circumstances, and when I determined I was not, I pushed his hand away, jumped up from the bed, and asked him what he thought he was doing, though it was more like a scream. He apologized and started weeping. I was too aghast to discuss the situation and just told him to take me back to the home where I was staying. I saw Bud only two more times at family events before he died of colon cancer in 2007. Neither my sister nor I attended his funeral.

When I returned from the trip, I told only Sharylee and Irvin about the incident. Sharylee commented that this sort of thing happened a lot. I was hoping for more support than that. My husband's reaction was much stronger: he wanted to kill him. Eventually he calmed down, and the matter rarely came up again. I had grown up in a world that thought the victim was somehow responsible for these incidents, and I couldn't help but believe it was partially true of me. After all, I did have a lot to drink and I went to his hotel room—and no such thing had happened to my sister.

For many years afterward I questioned myself. Had I been careless and somehow given him the idea that I had asked for it? But he was my father, even though he took few responsibilities in that regard. Should you have to be wary of your father? Shouldn't that be considered a different relationship than with other men? Shouldn't you have the right to feel safe even if he was a lousy father? The questions still race through my brain.

That was not the only time I have been sexually assaulted in my life, though it was one of the most difficult to live with. I have been sexually harassed at work, at school, and while on dates. I have never been raped, but I have run for my life on a couple of occasions to avoid it—or that's what I thought I was doing. Most of the time—I estimate at least fifteen or twenty times over the course of my life—swift hands have brushed across my breast or rear end. Sometimes I confronted the guys with the fast hands, sometimes not. One of the more shocking incidents happened while I was employed by the City of Houston as the Women's Advocate. A small group of us, all administrators working for equal rights in one way or another and all men except for me, were standing in a hallway visiting when a hand briefly slipped down the front of my dress and across my breast. I was quite sure that the hand belonged to the older man standing just to my left, but I was not absolutely certain. I looked up at him, but he was looking at others and his eyes did not meet mine. No one else seemed to be aware that anything unusual had taken place. It had happened unbelievably fast, and I was in a state of shock. I eased away and returned to my office, feeling my body temperature rising. I made a point to never stand beside him again.

I have great admiration for those women who have publicly stood up to abusers. I have thought a great deal about it in the last few years, questioning my decision not to say anything. The only excuse I have is that I felt humiliated, feared I would be blamed, and just wanted to get away and forget about it. Of course, I was never completely able to.

I have had two really terrifying experiences. One evening, when I was in high school, I was returning home from a friend's house. It was late evening, so quite dark. I was hurrying down the sidewalk toward my house when a car heading in the opposite direction pulled up beside me. He reached across the passenger side, rolled down the window, and asked me a question. I didn't understand what he said, so I walked closer to the car, asking him to repeat what he said. His question was, "Can you see what I'm playing with?" It took me a couple of seconds to realize what was going on. On my side of the street were a baseball diamond and a community swimming pool. Neither were in use at the time, so the area was deserted. Still three blocks from my house, I started to run. The driver made a swift U-turn and began following me. Fortunately, I was close to an intersection and as I started to cross it, out of the corner of my eye I recognized my sister walking toward me about a block and a half away. I let out a scream at Sharylee, yelling, "Run, run, run, run!" while running toward her. The car had turned the corner to follow me. Sharylee picked up my sense of terror and began running in the direction she had been coming from. I caught up to her, still screaming. Apparently the driver noticed that I had found a companion, for he turned his car around and took off. When I reached her, Sharylee had acquired my near state of panic. Once the car had gone, I explained what had happened and we calmed down a bit as we walked home.

We had always been taught that some men were dangerous and that young girls needed to be cautious. We did not expand our interpretation of what had happened beyond our having the bad luck to encounter one of the creeps. From then on, every time I walked home alone, I started running at the ballpark and didn't stop until I got home. I guess I thought I would be less of a target while running than walking.

My second heart-stopping experience happened while I was the executive director of the Houston Area Women's Center. I got up about 5:30 each morning to run before I went to work. Usually it was still fairly dark at that time. I would run from my house to a running track not far away. One morning I was about halfway to the track when I noticed a red car pass by a couple of times. The third time, the car came to an abrupt halt on the opposite side of the two-lane street and a guy jumped out and ran toward me, leaving his car door open. I immediately took off screaming at the top of my lungs. I could hear him behind me and envisioned a hand grabbing me at any moment. Fortunately, someone responded to my earth-shattering screams, opening his front door and yelling, "Hey, what's going on out there?" As soon as he heard another man's voice, the potential attacker turned and headed back to his car. I stopped and talked to the person who had saved me. He asked if I wanted him to call the police, which I didn't.

Still feeling unnerved when I got to work that day, I asked the director of our rape crisis center if I could share the experience with her. She was a wonderful counselor, one whom I never thought I would have reason to need. At her suggestion, I sent in a written report to the police department. By this time I knew that these kinds of attacks were linked to the inferior status of women in our society. Just as some of the suffragists had warned, a great deal more needed to be done after the passage of the Nineteenth Amendment. Although some things had changed because of the suffrage movement and as a result of World War II, the bias against women was still deeply embedded in our culture.

3 Education

After the passage of the Nineteenth Amendment in 1920, had women taken full advantage of their ability to vote, to elect women to office, and to pass legislation beneficial to women, the history of gaining equality for women might have looked very different.

Of course, they did not do that and could not for multiple reasons. In 1920, most women had no experience with voting and little understanding of the political system and the potential power of their votes, nor did they have access to the resources necessary to act on their newly won political rights, such as seeking public office. Cultural norms and stereotypes continued to trap them into thinking that political leadership was a role for men, not women. The age-old forces of social class, education, race, ethnicity, and geographical location kept women divided. Some women had little desire to change their circumstances. Others dealt with unplanned and unwanted pregnancies, violent husbands, or families that refused to invest in and encourage their daughters as they did their sons, all of which worked against the promise of granting women the vote.

Not all women accepted these limitations. The League of Women Voters was established in 1920. In chapters organized throughout the country, they trained other women, familiarizing them with how to use and benefit from the political system. Very few women, however, took the next step and actually ran for office.

As valuable as the right to vote was, education was the key to opening the doors to a wide range of additional benefits for women. Although women were being educated long before they won the right to vote, on the whole that education was limited. Higher education, college and graduate school, was largely reserved for men who were providing for their families and filling civic and political leadership roles.

The responsibility of public education was left primarily to the states in terms of standards, funding, and requirements for graduation. An exception to this arrangement was made following World War II, when congress passed the Servicemen's Readjustment Act of 1944, better known as the GI Bill. The bill provided veterans the opportunity to attend college by covering tuition (up to $500) as well as providing a living stipend, but according to the American Psychological Association, not all veterans benefitted equally. Women and African Americans had a difficult time taking advantage of the opportunity. Gender and racial bias gave preference to white male veterans, which tended to crowd out others, particularly in the more prestigious schools. The ripple effect of that bias resulted in diminished achievement for women. Fewer women had opportunities to become members of faculties, which then had a negative result on women students.

Then in 1972, the federal government took a major step toward prohibiting educational discrimination on the basis of sex. Title IX of the Education Amendments Act stated, "No person in the United States shall, on the basis of sex, be excluded from participation in, be denied the benefits of, or be subjected to discrimination under any education program or activity receiving Federal financial assistance." People are most familiar with the law for the enormous impact it has had on women and sports. The law is much broader than that, but the positive effect it had on women in college athletics was huge.

Education before Title IX consisted of separate schools and classes for males and females, different counseling services, the banning of pregnant girls from educational institutions, the exclusion of women or the placing of a quota on the percentage of women who could enter higher education, and the prohibition of women from military training. Most schools either limited or excluded women from team sports. Women typically hit the glass ceiling when they applied for such administrative roles as principal or superintendent, as it was generally believed that women's mothering instincts made them best suited to teaching very young children at the grade school level.

My grandmother had completed high school and then took vocational training in telegraphy, and my grandfather had made it through part of elementary school. Neither educational level was particularly unusual for people born in the nineteenth century. Two of their sons had some college education, but neither graduated. Their youngest son had a couple of years of college, but dropped out to seek employment, get married, and have children. Aside from the wartime interruptions, lack of money played a huge role in the inability to benefit more from education. Perhaps more importantly, decent paying jobs that did not require a college education were still available, at least for the men in my family. By the 1960s that had changed, and it changed particularly for women. In 1966, I was the first person in my family to earn a college degree.

I had no idea what benefits education would ultimately provide for my life. It took me a long time to grasp the true value of education and to recognize it as a tremendous gift that brought dramatic improvements and joy to the quality of my life. It has provided me a richness that far surpasses material gains, although I must admit that financial security comes much easier with a strong educational background.

I am ashamed to say that many of my early years of education were largely wasted due to my complete lack of appreciation for learning. My goal was always to complete the assignment, pass the test, finish the grade, and graduate. It had little to do with the value of gaining new knowledge. I didn't like the work involved and I didn't like the anxiety it caused. For me, the educational process was often a burdensome experience, and I could not grasp how it would benefit my future.

That said, not quite all of my early education affected me in the same way. From geography and history, I learned how to learn—at least enough to pass most tests. One of the most valuable skills I picked up was communicating in public. I had a wonderful teacher in the seventh grade who taught speech and drama. I have benefitted from that single junior high school class my entire life.

Not everything I learned was helpful. Everywhere I turned—at school, at home, and in popular culture—the stereotypes of males and females were enforced. Boys and men were stronger, more courageous, more willing to take risks, and better leaders, whereas women were weak, insecure, domestic, and dependent on men. For the most part, females were simply invisible in all aspects of my formal education. If a woman were less than a queen, it was likely she would never be mentioned in my school lessons, regardless of what she accomplished in life. Insofar as women's organizations and activism, the seventy-two-year-long suffrage movement received the most coverage in textbooks, but, according to a study by Kellian Clink at Minnesota State University, students were lucky to see but a brief paragraph about it. Women's role in prohibition received even less coverage, and usually the emphasis was on their apparent prudishness, with no discussion of the suffering that families experienced when the main breadwinner and the one who controlled the basic rights of all family members was a drunk.

My political thoughts were largely patterned after my grandmother's, who, as a conservative Republican, was a strong believer in the responsibility of individuals to take care of themselves and was largely hostile to government services. Work hard and you get ahead was the dominant political philosophy of the family. It made sense to me, although I am not quite sure why—my family certainly worked hard, but they never seemed to get ahead.

Making our way to college was no easy feat for my sister and me. Since she was a year ahead of me in school, Sharylee faced the problems first. We both had worked part-time in high school and saved some money. My fifty cents an hour as a stock clerk did not allow for much in savings. Our grandmother saved dimes from the grocery money, which was the best she could do to help out. Our grandfather simply ignored the matter. Partial scholarships helped. Sharylee was an excellent student who graduated second in her high school class, earning a half-tuition scholarship to the University of Tulsa. The two boys who graduated just ahead as well as just behind her all received full-tuition scholarships to Ivy League universities. While college counseling was available to the boys, our high school gave no information to Sharylee about the steps necessary to obtain scholarships or seek entrance to universities. If girls' parents weren't knowledgeable about or interested in assisting their daughters' college education, they usually didn't get one.

Besides the cost, travel also proved to be a major challenge. Sharylee luckily received a ride to the University of Tulsa her first year from a relative who lived in Tulsa but had been visiting in Billings. The next year we managed it together. We had two automobiles at home. One was fairly new, and the other one, a 1949 Pontiac, was a piece of worn-out junk. We asked our grandfather if we could take the Pontiac. He refused, saying that it was not safe to drive, as it was about to throw a rod and probably wouldn't make it to the city limits of Billings. I had no idea what "throwing a rod" meant. His assessment would probably have had a greater impact on us if we'd had more reason to trust him. We told our grandmother we were taking the car anyway. She knew next to nothing about automobiles and did not discourage us. My aunt (grandfather's sister) bought us two used tires. We made our move while he was away, and the beat-up Pontiac carried us all the way to Tulsa, Oklahoma.

My first year in college at the University of Tulsa was essentially a waste. I do not even remember the classes I took except for typing and shorthand, which I believed would help me get a job. Most of the girls at the University of Tulsa took those business courses as well because they, too, understood that some type of secretarial employment probably represented at least their short-term destiny. They were in college for much the same reason I was—it was what middle-class women who could manage it did until they married. I had no particular enthusiasm for marriage, but I couldn't see a real career in my future either other than secretarial work. There were no women role models who could give me ideas for what other paths to take.

I do not fault the professors for my failure to receive more benefit from their courses. As I mentioned previously, I had little appreciation for the value of education and the benefits it could provide. I had a very narrow understanding of why I was at the university in the first place. I felt truly lost.

Adding to the confusion in my life, just before Thanksgiving we received notice that my grandmother was gravely ill and that we should come to see her, probably for the last time. Her youngest son, Carol, who lived in Tulsa with his family, loaned us his station wagon to drive to Denver, and another family member paid for our plane tickets from Denver to Billings. My grandmother was in the hospital in Billings and had already lost much of her alertness. We stayed in our house, where our grandfather was now living by himself, but things did not go well there. He was angry that we had not remained in Billings to take care of our grandmother. After a few days we packed up our things and each moved to the home of a friend.

Our grandmother remained in a state of minimal consciousness. Sharylee and I began to feel pressed to return to school after missing a number of classes, plus we both had part-time jobs as well, and, so, lacking any other options, we headed back to Tulsa. We flew to Denver, where we had left Carol's car parked at the airport. We traded driving responsibilities and each kept her foot planted heavily on the accelerator. Shortly after we crossed the Oklahoma border, with Sharylee driving, the car jerked to the right, off the road, and rolled into farmland. I was thrown out of the car and seriously injured. There were no seat belts in 1958. Sharylee managed to stay in the car, where she was badly bruised but suffered no serious injuries. I, however, was lying in a field with a brain concussion, scalp lacerations, and broken bones in my back and chest. Fortunately, in a few minutes, another car stopped to offer help. The couple drove on to the nearest town to report the accident and send an ambulance back to us. (Of course, there were no cell phones in 1958!) I was in the hospital for several weeks. I came out with a shaved head and a large back brace. I was not a happy eighteen-year-old.

Carol had warned us that the wheel bearings were going out on the station wagon, so we should take it easy. What took the car off the road, we were never sure, but it gave us the opportunity to sue Carol's insurance company, which we did with Carol's full support. We settled for $3,000. We thought we were rich! We spent $1,000 on medical bills, $1,000 on the purchase of a used automobile, some on tuition, and the rest was ours to live on. We were in such dire need of money that it was almost worth the suffering we had to endure to get it.

When we originally left for Tulsa we knew that our grandmother was very ill. She had suffered from cancer for many years but had somehow managed to keep living. Her illness and pain had lasted for so long that, to me, it had become a grim state of normality. She told us that she was determined to live long enough to not only see Sharylee and me go to college but also to see us living independently. It was remarkable to see a person have that kind of control over their own life and death, but it was because she did not trust our grandfather to be in charge of our lives—a prospect that terrified my sister and me as well. Our grandmother died after Sharylee and I had returned to Tulsa, shortly before Christmas. We had only a small amount of money at the time, and I had just been released from the hospital, so there was no possibility of us returning to Billings for her funeral. It was a sad ending for me, my sister, and our grandmother. She was a brave and devoted parent. My grandmother was, for all practical purposes, my only parent, and that was a terrible loss. On the other hand, I experienced a sense of relief that her many years of terrible pain and suffering as the cancer wreaked havoc on her body were over. With her death plus alienation from my grandfather, I felt removed from Billings as a home. There was no other home to replace it.

In the summer after my first and Sharylee's second year of college, Sharylee managed to find both of us jobs in a laundry in one of the lodges in Yellowstone National Park. To travel there, we once again relied on our old '49 Pontiac, which had been sitting dead for months on the curb outside our dorm. With the assistance of some male friends, we were able to get it running again, so the two of us headed off to Yellowstone. It was a nerve-wracking trip. We each held our breath every time we tried to start it, then once it was running we lived in fear that it would be the last time. Yellowstone became the Pontiac's graveyard—not too bad considering our grandfather's prediction that it would not make it past the city limits of Billings.

The summer of 1958 in Yellowstone was mostly a relaxed and joyful experience. By then, although my hair was unusually short, I was no longer bald, and, I, probably unwisely, had abandoned the back brace early on in the trunk of the Pontiac. There were young people in Yellowstone from all over the country, mostly college kids, happy to do the mundane jobs available for very little pay in the park. We had a dorm to live in rent-free and food to eat. I dreaded the end of the summer and the return to what I thought was a purposeless life as a student at the University of Tulsa. But before I could deal with that, we had to find transportation out of the park and back to Tulsa. With college kids from all over the country working in Yellowstone Park for the summer, it wasn't long before we managed to find a ride.

When I walked back into the women's dorm in Tulsa, the dread became too much to bear. I knew I had to make a change in my life. I quit school. Making good use of my business courses, I found a job with Avis Rent-a-Car. At the time, the company's headquarters were in Tulsa. The pay was decent enough for me to afford to rent a one-bedroom apartment, which I shared with my sister and a friend. My main task was typing detailed financial reports, as there were no computers or word processors available at that time. I later became a car rental clerk. The work, paycheck, and personal freedom appealed to me at that time. Although I was largely oblivious to the situation, the workforce at Avis was highly segregated by gender and race. Women worked in the financial affairs department except for the manager, who was male. Managers of the rental operations in all locations were male. Rental clerks were mostly female. Mechanics, car washers, and other maintenance workers were males, mostly African Americans.

Within my first year of working for Avis, Irvin was transferred in to be the city manager of the car rental services in Tulsa. I was twenty and he was twenty-nine. We married in July of 1960, shortly after he was transferred to St. Louis, where we moved into an apartment. I began looking for a job as a secretary, searching the want ads of the newspaper, which in the 1960s reflected the segregation in the workforce. To find a job for myself, I searched under "help wanted female." Had I been African American I would have looked under "help wanted colored." Most job opportunities for females were for secretary or clerk positions.

When I made phone inquiries, I was asked about my marital status, about having children or plans for having children, even about what kind of birth control I was using. Not until 1978 would there be legal protections against this kind of discrimination. The policy of most companies at the time was to terminate the employment of pregnant women, especially those who had some contact with the public, such as receptionists. It was assumed that once a woman became pregnant, she would devote herself to her real job in domestic life.

I was hired by the accounting firm Peat, Marwick, Mitchell and

Co. as the office secretary. All accountants were male and had private offices, whereas all the secretaries and clerks were female and had desks in common rooms. From where I sat, I saw the people who came in as job seekers. One day a young woman applied for an accounting job. She held an accounting degree and, as I found out later, had graduated at the top of her class. She was told that the firm did not hire women as accountants, but they offered her a job in the company's bookkeeping department at considerably less pay. After I got to know her I learned that she had taken the book-keeping job because not hiring women accountants was common practice among all large accounting firms. I asked her if she knew why. She said the explanation she was given was that clients did not like to have women going through their books. She left after a few months.

Bored and restless with the stuffiness of the firm, I left shortly after she did and took a job with the sales branch of a liquor manu-facturing firm as a secretary, like the other four women in the firm. All the men in their private offices were in sales. I was beginning to see the future, and it was not bright. There were few promotional opportunities for the jobs women held and, thus, little possibility for increasing salaries. Also, there was a class status. The men were in the top ranks with authority over the women. Having or not having a degree made little difference in the status of women. Women with degrees tended to make a little more money than those without, although they were doing the same work in most cases.

I was growing more and more unhappy with the prospects of my work life. I began to recognize that I had ambitions, but I wasn't sure in what direction to turn. Irvin was sympathetic and urged me to return to college. He had more confidence in me than I did in myself. Every time I thought about it I remembered my failure at the University of Tulsa. I had no desire to repeat that. Irvin, not having finished college, was conscious of the limitations it had placed on his life, although he had done quite well in the car rental business. I finally decided to follow his suggestion, enrolling at Washington University in St. Louis. My majors were history and secondary education. The ideas then about reasonable majors for woman were very limited, but I was exceedingly conscious of my desire to find a job and earn my own income.

This time around, I desperately wanted to be successful, so I really dug into my studies. One of my first courses was on logic. It truly blew me away. Learning about the process of reasoning and thinking was exhilarating. I don't think I had even heard of the concept of logic before I took the course. One course after another opened my eyes to the way the world functioned. My grades were not superb but they steadily improved; besides, my grades did not begin to reflect the pleasure and pride I took in the experience. I wasn't too keen on some of the required courses, yet a course on the Socratic method of teaching utterly changed the way I thought. The instructor was both wonderful and relentless—I would leave class with my hands shaking from the stress of learning to defend my position.

When I was within one semester of graduating from Washington University, Irvin was transferred from St. Louis to Houston. In the car rental business, a transfer was tantamount to a promotion. Neither of us considered his refusing it. After all, he was the breadwinner and I still had a hard time taking myself seriously. I could not conceive of staying in St. Louis without him to finish my degree. After the move, I enrolled in the University of Houston, where I needed thirty course hours to graduate. Since I had already completed most of the required courses, I began taking classes in political science, a subject in which I had always had an interest. The high quality of the political science department in Houston almost made up for my disappointment at leaving Washington University. I soon found that UH was not as demanding, and my grades improved considerably, which pleased me. By the end of the year I had made up my mind to try for a master's degree in political science. I didn't think beyond that because I still didn't have enough confidence in my academic ability to conjure a vision of myself acquiring a PhD.

The most significant aspect of graduate school for me was learning about research that explored and explained group behavior. It was all so new to me. I had never thought about how or where knowledge originated or changed. I guess I thought there was a standard bag of knowledge that was passed on from one generation to the next. Those who were considered well educated knew more about what was in the bag than others. Never in my wildest dreams did I think I could be a creator of new knowledge through my own research.

In the field of political science, research tended to focus on human behaviors in politics: why people believed what they believed, where they gained their beliefs, why they acted as they did, and what and who tended to motivate them. Important paths of inquiry into these questions were sociological characteristics such as age, race, ethnicity, income, gender, and education.

Studying these connections fascinated me, probably because this knowledge had a powerful impact on my insight into my own life. My thinking had previously rested on individualism. Now I could see that our family was the product of a culture; that group thinking and group behaviors developed from educational levels, from wealth, from physical appearance, and from religion; that our outlook, beliefs, and ideologies were passed from group to group, usually starting with the family. I began to recognize that changes in those beliefs and behaviors required some kind of intervention, such as college life, experiences with government policies, employment or unemployment, and a host of other circumstances. I realized I was changing as a result of my education, that some of my old beliefs were giving way to these new sources of knowledge. One can resist new knowledge, but for me it was powerfully influential. More and more, I felt a growing distance from the influence of my family, religion, and political beliefs. I changed from Republican to a Democrat when I realized that party provided a better explanation of the political actions and public policies that I found valuable. Liberalism made more sense to me than conservatism. Science took over where religion had been.

I couldn't resist sharing my new thoughts with Irvin. He didn't always agree with me, and we spent many hours talking, debating, and sometimes arguing about all I was learning in my new world. When we got together with friends or family members, it was the same. I am sure I exhausted people. I completed my master's degree in political science at the University of Houston, then I taught for a year at the university's downtown branch, which mainly offered introductory courses for people just entering college. That teaching experience made it obvious that my knowledge was still limited.

Irvin was transferred to the Avis headquarters in Long Island,

New York, in 1969. It was an exciting move for me in many ways. I was accepted into the political science doctoral program at New York University and, at age thirty, began working on a PhD. I had the good fortune to receive a full scholarship with a living stipend from the National Institute of Mental Health. In retrospect, it's hard to believe my good fortune. I had learned of the fellowship program in materials that were sent to me when I was accepted to NYU. Its purpose was to train political science graduate students in health and mental health policy for a period of four years. The faculty member who was the administrator of the grant, Dr. Ralph Straetz, was in charge of selecting the fellows each year. There were only about seven to ten students in the program at any given time. It sounded like a great opportunity.

I was interviewed by Dr. Straetz and was accepted. Exactly how I was granted this jewel of a fellowship, I will never know. There were only two women, including me, in the class that I entered in 1970. I recently asked my colleague, Marilyn Falik, who knew Dr. Straetz better than I did, if she had any thoughts on why, as women, we were selected. She speculated that he was very fair and supportive of women. There were few women in the entire political science graduate program, which meant there was not a large pool to choose from. It's also possible that the grant itself required a diverse student body.

It would have been nearly impossible for me to complete the PhD program without assistance because NYU was outrageously expensive. We lived on Long Island, but my courses were in the Greenwich Village section of Manhattan, meaning that for the first time in my life I had to use public transportation. Living in the New York area was an education unto itself. NYU was alive with activity and protests during the Vietnam War. The student body was incredibly diverse. It was an eye-opening experience for me, but after the newness of everything wore off, I settled into a routine of several years of reading and writing papers and commuting on the Long Island Railroad and New York City subways for several hours a day.

Something new that grabbed my attention were articles in various NYU media outlets about the activities of a women's rights or feminist movement, which immediately intrigued me. I had not been aware of any sort of women's rights movement in

Houston, but at NYU organizations were forming and issues such as violence against women, self-defense, and abortion rights were being discussed and debated. Demonstrations were common, and these activities were covered by campus media.

In my studies up to that point, of all the factors that were acknowledged as causes of difference in groups of people, gender had been rarely mentioned, or it had been a joke to throw into an otherwise boring lecture. I do recall a question from the professor of my first graduate course at the University of Houston: "Why is it that women do better in undergraduate school and men exceed in graduate school?" The class responded with silence. He answered his own question: "Because women are not as capable of conceptualizing and generalizing data. They are better at memorizing facts, which are the demands of undergraduate school. Men, on the other hand, can cope with large amounts of data, conceptualize, and develop theories." I was stunned and terrified at the same time. What if this is true? I asked myself. I'm defeated before I even start.

I began paying closer attention to the material I was required to read for my graduate courses at UH and NYU and found little to nothing there about women's issues. I couldn't even write papers on the subject because there was no foundation or factual basis with which to start. I began to wonder why this lack of information hadn't been obvious to me before. Attitudes were starting to change at NYU. The women in my classes would speak up when a professor made a sexist remark. There had been no women faculty members in either the UH or NYU political science departments; the pressure for change was coming from the students, primarily the female students.

In 1972, I reached the point of selecting a topic for a dissertation. I was fascinated with the topic of women in politics. I started searching for articles that had already been written so that I could add new knowledge to the subject through my research. I developed a kind of sick feeling when I discovered that almost no research had been done. I went back as far as the relevant political science journals were available and found a total of about five articles. It was not enough to provide the background I needed. Seeking advice, I turned to the faculty members—all male—on my dissertation committee. Not only did I not receive help, I received discouragement. The reason given to me for this lack of research was that there was nothing of importance to say. Women, if they did anything political, I was told, followed the directions of their husbands. The fact that I could find very limited research on the topic proved their point that there was nothing worth researching.

Rather than discouraging me, they made me even more determined. I decided on the subject of why women were not as politically involved as men. It seemed to be considered a given that women had no interest in politics, so the obvious question was why not? Finally, I got a break. One of the members of my dissertation committee suggested I get in touch with a faculty member in the sociology department. He explained that she was focusing her research on women and would like to help me. She turned out to be a godsend, guiding me to academic articles in sociology and psychology. It became so clear to me then: The socialization of women directed them away from leadership roles, especially larger leadership roles in society. Women were traditionally socialized to serve men and to bear and rear children. Many of the qualities required to be a political leader—independence, self-confidence, assertiveness—were antithetical to the socialization of women.

The question that arose next was why had women worked so hard to get the vote? According to the literature on the suffrage movement, a majority of the suffragists had little aspiration to seek public office. Their strategy for gaining political power was focused on having and using the right to vote. The ability to exercise power through their votes would force the men who were in office to pay attention to women's needs and moral standards.

My initial research on why women were still largely disinclined to run for office revealed that the discouraging nature of women's socialization was still largely in force. Manhood involved leadership; womanhood involved supporting men. For my dissertation, I turned the question around and asked why, in fact, some women do run for office. I titled my dissertation "The Politics of Female Socialization." In the 1972 election, sixty women ran for state and national office within the New York City and Long Island area compared to hundreds of men. I personally interviewed all but a few of those women, asking about their backgrounds and motivation for running for office.

My hypothesis was that these women candidates, who challenged political traditions by running for office, would consider themselves feminists and were motivated to run by their belief in women's equality. I was surprised and disappointed to learn that this was largely not the case. The majority of the candidates had some feminist leanings, but for the most part, they were civic leaders who had been asked by the parties to run. Further, they had almost no chance of winning the seats they were running for because they were in gerrymandered districts that strongly favored the opposition party. They had been intentionally recruited by the minority parties to run in these hopeless districts. It wasn't that the parties wanted them to lose, but with a negative outcome likely, parties had been unable to recruit strong, knowledgeable, male candidates willing to make the sacrifice. Most of the women had never been candidates before and were largely naïve about what it took to win. From the parties' point of view this was a benefit—by recruiting women just as the women's movement was getting underway, they were betting on the remote possibility of women voters crossing party lines to vote for a woman candidate. The parties had nothing to lose by this because they were going to lose the seat anyway. The women candidates in these hopeless districts told me they had been promised help from the parties—money, volunteers, guidance—none of which ever materialized. Most of the fifty-six women who lost ended the races feeling angry and misused. I doubt if any of them ever ran for office again.

Of the four women who won, two were incumbents: Bella Abzug and Shirley Chisholm, who both served in the US House of Representatives. The two other winners were elected to their state senate and continued on to successful lives in politics. Like their male counterparts, these four women knew their way around politics and ran only in districts where there was a strong possibility of winning. They knew that winning elective office was a dogfight for anyone, male or female, and they were prepared to engage in it. They also knew the roadblocks facing women, and they were prepared to face them.

This research project for my dissertation was a tremendous, eye-opening education for me. My original goal for earning a PhD had been to teach in a university. Although I did not abandon that goal, over the course of my research I had become a strong feminist and was no longer satisfied to be an academic observer. I wanted to be an activist. I wanted to change the conditions that shrunk women's lives, ideas, and opportunities. While I was writing my dissertation, I joined a local chapter of the National Organization for Women and would later open another chapter. Life was suddenly very exciting.

4 Women's Advocate

Earning a PhD was an accomplishment I felt honored to have achieved. For me, though, it was even more than pride in myself, because the process, primarily the experience of researching and writing my dissertation, changed my life. The challenges were not over, however. My goal was to be a university professor. I wanted a career where I could apply what I had learned. This next step became unexpectedly complicated when a few months before I completed and defended my dissertation Irvin had a major heart attack. He was in the hospital for several weeks, and at times his life was seriously at risk. Not having any idea of what might come next, I continued to work on my dissertation and be involved in the chapter of NOW that I had helped found. Irvin's health finally began to improve. I defended my dissertation and it appeared that life was going to carry on.

Though jobs were very tight when I was finishing my PhD, I received an offer to join the political science faculty of Lehigh University in Lehigh, Pennsylvania. Irvin also received an offer—the chance to return to Houston as the city manager for Avis, just as his health was improving. It became one of those situations professional couples more and more commonly faced. The social system was designed for husbands to be the primary breadwinners, but women slowly began gaining career opportunities, which sometimes resulted in couples being pulled in two directions. On the one hand, I longed to start my own career as a tenure track faculty member. On the other hand, Irvin had worked for Avis for almost twenty years. His health was uncertain, and of all the places he had worked, he had a particular attachment to Houston. In many ways,

I did too. We had spent some happy years there and were familiar with the city. The weight was on the side of Houston. Once again, I started searching for a job.

The relocation issue was only the beginning of what we had yet to learn about a marriage based on equality. I knew considerably more about what that wasn't than what it was. Little had changed in our personal lives over the course of my education. I had accepted the notion that I was fortunate to have the opportunity to take on the PhD program and commit a large amount of time to it, but I had done so while continuing to do the vast amount of domestic work. Occasionally, I would bring it up with Irvin and get a little help with the housework, laundry, cooking, and shopping for a short period of time, then it was back to business as usual. His job's heavy demand on his time was part of the problem. His lifetime of believing that his employment should be our priority was the other part. His income was always considerably more than mine, and with money went power. I loved Irvin and he loved me, but as a white Southern male from Augusta, Georgia, he had acquired many expectations early in his life that never changed. In my mind, we clearly had a long way to go in this matter of equality.

I studied other married students who were getting their PhDs to see how they managed the distribution of work. Most of the students were male and, if they were married, typically their wives held jobs that supported them. The long-range plans were that the husbands would finish their degrees, get jobs, and become the major breadwinners. Their primary task while in school was to dedicate their time to their academic work. Their wives handled most of the domestic affairs and children, if they had any. There was one other married woman in the program. She talked with me about the difficulties she had encountered. Her husband's complaint was that he wanted her to be routinely available to help meet the demands of his life. I was glad that Irvin was very proud and encouraging of my ambitions. Yet he was still reluctant or unwilling to share domestic responsibilities.

After we returned to Houston, I began a search for either a teaching position or an administrative position in a university. There weren't many options. The University of Houston and Rice University were the only major local universities. I didn't apply to

Rice, thinking that I would not meet their standards. I had not yet published anything, although I was working on an article from my dissertation. I didn't think I had much chance at the University of Houston because I had received my bachelor's and master's degrees from there, and universities didn't usually hire their former students. The remaining options were mainly community colleges. It came as a nice surprise when I received an offer from the chair of the department of political science at the University of Houston to be a visiting assistant professor. A visiting position usually meant a one-year contract that could be terminated at the end of each academic year. I accepted it, thinking that this might lead to a full-time, tenure-track position, which had the benefit of providing a considerably greater amount of job security. I can't say I enjoyed the teaching. I was still quite unsure of myself as a teacher.

Toward the end of my second year of teaching, the position opened for the Women's Advocate for the City of Houston, via the mayor's office. The position had been created as a result of a strong lobbying effort by the Women's Political Caucus, a women's rights organization created to perform the kinds of political activities that a nonprofit like NOW was prohibited from doing. Initially, the proposal for the position went nowhere due to its unpopularity with the conservative mayor at the time, Louie Welch. However, an election was coming up in the fall of 1973 for mayor and city council in Houston, and Welch was not planning to run again. A young, change-oriented candidate, Fred Hofheinz, whose father had also been mayor in the past, was in the running. He made a strong appeal to women and minorities, and he committed to feminist groups to support the creation of the Office of Women's Advocate.

Hofheinz won the election and in March 1974 he appointed the first Women's Advocate, Frances "Poppy" Northcutt. The first female engineer to work in NASA's Mission Control, first on Apollo 8 and then on several other missions, Northcutt was a leader in the women's rights movement and actively involved in NOW and the Women's Political Caucus. In his letter of appointment to Northcutt, the mayor stated that the office would be "a forum for the expression of women's concerns." Northcutt served for nineteen months as Women's Advocate. In her final report, she listed accomplishments that included tripling the number of women in the police force, changing the dress code policy for female city employees, initiating city-paid medical examinations for rape victims, and instigating extensive data analysis and reporting on the under-representation of women in city government.

The matter of the women's dress code was a good example of some of the humiliating circumstances that female city employees had had to tolerate. In researching her master's thesis on the Office of Women's Advocate, University of Houston graduate student Judith Jett Hendricks uncovered a 1973 memo from Mayor Louie Welch addressed to all female employees mandating that if they wore pant-suits to work, as that clothing item had just recently been allowed for women, their jackets must reach to the bottom of their rear ends. Some of the other instructions included, "Do not wear pantsuits if your figure exceeds size 14," and, "Finally, take a good look in the mirror. If you have any reservations about the pantsuit, don't wear it. It is not worth the embarrassment of being called on the carpet."

After Northcutt left the position, it remained vacant for seven months, but not forgotten. Women's rights groups pressed hard to have a new Women's Advocate appointed, concerned that the mayor might drop the position rather than deal with the political dynamics surrounding it. While it was vacant, opponents of the women's movement had time to organize and make their case to the conservative city council members that there was no need for another Women's Advocate. The debate over filling the position of the Women's Advocate overlapped with an intense struggle over the passage of the Equal Rights Amendment. Even though Texas was one of the first states to ratify the ERA, opposition within the state was hoping to have that ratification rescinded. There was no precedent addressing the legality of rescinding a constitutional amendment once it had been ratified by a state. Many legal minds challenged such a move as unconstitutional, but the ERA's oppo-nents were not easily discouraged.

I was aware of the opposition that was brewing to eliminate the position of the Women's Advocate. I saw the position as a critical part of the women's movement in Houston, and I was willing to take risks to keep it filled. The position had great appeal to me person-ally because I was drawn to organizing and to activism on behalf of women. After relocating to Houston, I had become involved with the Houston chapter of NOW just as I had been involved in Long Island. With that experience plus a PhD in political science, I thought I should be in a favorable position for the job. I was right.

On May 17, 1976, I was hired by Mayor Fred Hofheinz to be the Women's Advocate for the City of Houston. My office was located in the Affirmative Action Division of the Mayor's Office. The Office of the Women's Advocate consisted of one person and a half-time secretary. No one knew what I was actually supposed to do, and the division head paid little attention to me. Like Northcutt, what I did in the position was very much up to me.

I quickly learned that it was largely a token position and that I had very little real power. I initially focused on discrimination against women city employees, but even when I received

Houston Breakthrough

Vol. 1, No. 6   JUNE - JULY 1976

COMPLIMENTARY COPY
For Future Issues
PLEASE SUBSCRIBE   50¢

Women's Advocate named

by Gay Cosgriff

Houston's new Women's Advocate, Dr. Nikki Van Hightower, sees herself as just that -- an advocate for all the women of Houston.

Most of her energies will be directed towards getting women who are employed by the city into decision-making positions, and promoting qualified women within their departments. "I think if you saw the way jobs are sex-segregated in City Hall," Van Hightower says, "you would see that women are automatically put into the lower status, clerical kinds of jobs."

Van Hightower, formerly an assistant professor in political science at the University of Houston, was appointed last month by Mayor Fred Hofheinz to fill the office which had been vacant for seven months.

Since the City of Houston is currently experiencing a hiring

Department officially has authority in hiring and promotion, in practice each department head has tremendous autonomy, which is why Van Hightower feels that a merit system is essential to ensure promotion of qualified women. There is no female equivalent of the 'good-old-boy' club.

"I believe that without an outside, objective criterion for hiring and promotion, women are stifled in their desire to advance themselves," she says. In the short time she has been in office, Van Hightower has received a number of calls from women employed by the city who feel that hard work and dedication do not win them the promotions they deserve-- rather, they are penalized for being 'aggressive'. "Women still are clearly stereotyped in terms of what jobs they hold," she states.

Since her appointment, Van Hightower has been spending

Council member Homer Ford stated, "I see the office of Women's Advocate as an overlapping of services provided by others in the affirmative action office and civil service."

"The city has been doing a good job of hiring women," said Council member Louis Macey.

"A Women's Advocate is not any more necessary than a man's advocate," believes Council member Frank Mancuso. "It is a waste of taxpayers' money and I see no need for it."

Van Hightower replied, "Men already have advocates--they are well represented in all the highest levels of city government. They do not have the problem of under-representation that women have."

Van Hightower is emphatic in saying that she sees herself as being instrumental in raising the consciousness of city officials. "Consciousness raising with city

Announcement of Nikki's appointment as Women's Advocate on the front page of Houston Breakthrough, *vol. 1, no. 6 (June–July 1976). Courtesy of* Houston Breakthrough *magazine.*

complaints of discrimination, I had no authority to resolve the problems. I could make requests and send in reports, which I did, but it was likely nothing would come of them. When women reported discrimination or sexual harassment, I contacted their supervisors if they wanted me to, but sometimes the supervisor was the problem. Filing a complaint to a supervisor could be risky. My intervention could jeopardize women's jobs.

To provide a basis for making claims of unfair treatment and discrimination, I began working on an extensive data analysis comparing the status of the pay and job titles of female and male city employees. My first step was to make a request for personnel data from the head of the Affirmative Action Division. He declined, telling me that my position did not qualify me to have access to personnel data. I was stunned. I pointed out that everyone in the division had access to that data. They had to have it to do their jobs. His response was that I was not technically part of the Affirmative Action Division—they had just needed a department somewhere to house me.

I informed him that I intended to go to the mayor about the matter. He gave a laugh and told me that he didn't think I would get anywhere. Before I'd had time to speak with the mayor, one of the division employees, Raul Castillo, an administrative assistant who compiled the city's federally required employment reports, told me that he had access to the data and would provide me with anything I needed. He shared some other interesting information: before I had arrived on the job, the division head had warned him and other employees not to provide me with any personnel data I requested, or anything else for that matter. With Raul's assistance, I completed the study showing essentially the same bias that my predecessor, Poppy, had documented and sent it to the mayor and to the division head who had withheld the information. Nothing was ever said, and nothing was ever done.

There was a high degree of sex segregation in city government, and with it were wide variations in pay. Even when women and men performed the same duties, they were often given different job titles and paid differently. For instance, men who were titled "accountant" performed essentially the same duties as women who were titled "bookkeeper," but the men were paid significantly more.

That structural bias had been around for a very long time and little had been done about it. The different job titles kept the city fairly safe from the Equal Pay Act, a federal law.

I wrote about all of these concerns for a special issue of the City of Houston employee newsletter. The special issue, dedicated to women employees, introduced the International Women's Year Conference (IWY) coming to Houston, and highlighted some of the successful women employees in Houston city government. My article was later included in the IWY National Conference proceedings.

> They are young, they are old, they come from diverse racial and ethnic backgrounds. Some are married, some divorced and raising their children by themselves and some are widowed. Women employees of Houston City Government, in fact, very much resemble the community they serve. Their changing ideas, status and goals reflect our own dynamic Houston.
>
> Women in Houston City Government are no longer willing to be locked into certain employment roles just because they happen to be members of the female sex, and these changed attitudes are slowly beginning to be reflected in statistical reports on employees. The percentage of women in the official/administrative job category has increased from 9% to 20.1% since 1973 and from 29.5% to 37.3% in the professional job category.
>
> Barriers to women have not totally disappeared, by any means. Old attitudes and traditions die hard and most of the City women are still employed in traditional female occupations (58% of all female City workers are employed in the office/clerical job category).
>
> There is a new awareness, however, growing among both workers and employers of the value of the traditional women's jobs and of the fact that compensation for these jobs should be in line with men's jobs which require similar levels of skills and experience.
>
> Women city employees, like all women, still have a long way to go before they reach full equality with men. But these employees are, in the words of the National Women's Conference, truly "Women on the move." It is therefore most

appropriate that this issue of City Magazine should be devoted
to them and to their vital contributions to the well-being of
all Houstonians, in conjunction with this historic event.

Like most local governments, the City of Houston was pressured to
establish an Affirmative Action Program, which it did in the early
1970s. Also like most state and local governments, women in the

Special issue of City Government Employee *magazine dedicated to*
women.

city government of Houston were under-hired, underpaid, routinely passed over for promotions, and subjected to sexual harassment. Sexual harassment was not acknowledged as a form of employment discrimination until 1980 when the Equal Employment Opportunity Commission (EEOC) officially declared it to be such.

The EEOC was created by the Civil Rights Act of 1964. In 1965, it was amended by Executive Order 11246, making affirmative action a condition of doing business with the federal government. For state and local governments, failure to comply raised the potential threat of losing federal funds. However, just because the affirmative programs were established did not mean they were conscientiously enforced. For that to happen, women had to gain enough clout to overcome what seemed like endless cultural barriers against supervising men and making and enforcing political policies.

A significant amount of my time was spent on the structural biases that affected many if not most working women. For instance, childcare was a major problem for many employees, particularly women. Another city employee joined me in conducting a childcare needs assessment study. Although evidence from the study indicated that childcare costs were a major drain on city salaries and that many children were at risk because childcare was not available or could not be afforded, the matter was largely ignored by city officials. After an analysis of the city's maternity policy and a subsequent consultation with the city legal department, the policy was found to be discriminatory. That finding was based on the benefits men received for major medical issues compared to the benefits for pregnant workers. City officials were advised of the findings. I also worked closely with the city attorney on a policy in the parks department that prohibited women from working outdoors, which many female employees wanted to do. We tried to eliminate that policy. Nothing changed.

All these issues had required a great deal of time and finesse on my part to gain permission to investigate the basis of the policies behind them. Changes to those policies would have provided significant benefits to employees and their families, but such issues tended to receive little media attention while other issues with far less potential impact on the lives of workers received more extensive coverage.

An example of an incident that really got under the skin of the council members arrived on my doorstep shortly after I took the position of Women's Advocate. It started with the donation of a statue of Confucius from the People's Republic of China with an inscription stating, "Men have their Respective Occupations and Women their Homes." It was placed in the main branch of the city library at the request of the city council members. In this case, the mayor's office sent the media over to my office for comments, which I was happy to give them. I said something about the inappropriateness of placing a statue bearing an inscription with such implications in a location where the majority of the employees were women. The *New York Times* described the affair: "It was Nikki Van Hightower, the city's official Advocate for Women's Rights who spotted the inscription on the base and quickly branded the Chinese sage 'the sexist of his time.'"

I spoke to the director of the Municipal Arts Commission, and he agreed that the statue with this inscription was inappropriate for city offices and that it should be placed somewhere else. I then contacted the mayor, and he also agreed it should be moved. Seventy-six female employees of the library system sent a letter of complaint about the statue. The matter of the statue received heavy media attention, leading to rants by many of the city council members, some of whom claimed that it was very possible for this to escalate into an international incident. It was hard for me to imagine what they expected a women's advocate to do if not to advocate for women. The council members despised my receiving media attention, and, unfortunately, the media only appeared to be interested in covering issues like the statue that could be made into a humorous story.

Regardless of the lack of real authority in the job, I strongly felt the pressure of the word "advocate" in my job title. Other people did as well. City workers and citizens took it very seriously, and my phone rang steadily with calls from people inside and outside city government. The expectations for what I could do were very high, much higher than the reality of what I actually could do.

One of the things I was able to accomplish that seemed most appreciated by women travelers was eliminating pay toilets from the women's bathrooms in the two Houston airports. The issue came to me in a very roundabout way. One day Irvin was having lunch with some of the Avis employees at the airport, where he spent quite a bit of time. One of the women complained that she had lost her key to the bathroom stalls; female employees at the airports received keys to allow them access to the pay toilets without charge, which, as I recall, was about twenty-five cents for everyone else. The male employees at the luncheon table asked what that was about. The men didn't have to pay. Thus, no keys were necessary for them. Since the conversation had not come up before, the women were not aware of this obnoxious act of discrimination. Irvin told me about the discussion when he came home that night. I contacted several media sources and by the next day the news had spread. It was a matter that caused a lot of heat among women, regardless of how they felt about the Women's Advocate. The council members were caught flatfooted. They tried to play it down as a silly thing on which the Women's Advocate was wasting taxpayer's money. That didn't work. Council members were hounded with calls, and letters to the editor flew in. There was no other choice; the coin boxes had to be removed. They were, but in the meanest way possible. The doors on all the women's bathroom stalls were removed for several days, then replaced with lockless doors for several more days before new locks, requiring no coins, were finally installed. I feel certain that all females who flew into the Houston airports at that time would be greatly annoyed to find that the demands of their bladders had contributed over $17,000 per year to the city's income.

It was one of those issues so touchy to women that the story spread around the country. Airports that still retained coin-operated locks on women's toilet stalls quickly replaced them. My sister, Sharylee, who lived in Santa Fe, New Mexico, at the time and who flew in and out of the Albuquerque airport, found the same situation there. She notified the Albuquerque media; no doubt many other women did likewise. The locks were soon removed. I had to laugh.

After about six months of wrestling with the city council, I refocused my attention to groups and individuals outside of city government. Judith Hendricks, the graduate student who was writing her master's thesis on the subject of the Office of the

Women's Advocate, asked me how I divided my time between requests from civilian groups and individuals and city employees. My response was, "Half and half. But now I'm spending more and more time on outside projects, mainly because the internal ones are hopeless . . . because I have no power . . ."

During one of the rallies on behalf of the Women's Advocate, a woman by the name of Phyllis Frye introduced herself to me and told her story as a transgendered person. She explained the hardships that she and other transgendered people suffered and that they lacked legal protections. She wanted me to understand the issue and help out as best I could. I listened carefully, though as the transgender issue was new to me at that time, I worried I didn't have much to offer. Ms. Frye turned out to be a very successful organizer for the rights of transgender people and women, not only in the Houston Area, but throughout the country. She earned a law degree, and was appointed as a municipal court judge in Houston by former mayor Annise Parker.

The positive support I received from the mayor, his staff, and the media seemed only to antagonize the city council members. As time went along the hostility of some of them became more open and vicious. As one council member said, "We don't need a women's advocate any more than we need a 'men's advocate.'" Of course, all seven council members were "men's advocates." They were not happy with the attention I was receiving from the press or with the possibility that I was stirring the political pot. At that point, no woman had ever been elected to a city government position in Houston and few ever ran. The council members did not like to think about the possibility of women as competitors.

One of my goals as I shifted direction more to outside projects was to mobilize citizens in the community to bring pressure on behalf of women both inside and outside of city government. I helped organize a large coalition of women's organizations, hoping that their voices would be added to my voice for change. We called the coalition the Women's Rights Coordinating Council (WRCC). It included more than forty women's organizations that were oriented to both feminist issues and civic affairs.

The first action of the WRCC was to hold an International Women's Year rally in front of city hall on March 5, 1977, to bring both the needs of women and the projects necessary to meet those needs to the attention of the public and city officials. The WRCC asked me to be the keynote speaker for the rally. In my address, I covered issues such as equal pay; health care, including reproductive rights; violence against women; and support of the Equal Rights Amendment. Following the rally, representatives from the WRCC were going to testify before the city council and request additional staff for the Office of the Women's Advocate in order to implement the proposed projects.

Before the WRCC could speak to the council, a protest group opposed to the Equal Rights Amendment and the legal right to abortion lodged their complaints. The council acted immediately, voting unanimously, with the exception of the mayor, to reduce the salary of the Women's Advocate to $1 per year. This action was clearly planned in advance as a way to humiliate me by telling the public I was worth only $1 per year.

I was stunned. I struggled to understand how anyone, much less an elected official, in the latter half of the twentieth century could find such an action appropriate. I wondered if it had been meant as some kind of joke. When I spoke to the mayor, my impression was that he found it kind of humorous. He explained that the action had undoubtedly been pre-planned. It wasn't as if there were a groundswell of hostility toward me. Quite the opposite—only seven citizens had showed up to lodge their complaints. He said that the council could not legally implement the change. The city controller, also elected, refused to make the change in the budget. So, as it turned out, my salary did not change.

What did happen was a huge reaction from the community. Demonstrations were held in front of city hall, literature was distributed, and the media had a field day with the story, all of which reflected very badly on the city council members. Though my office was salvaged, this conflict was not what I had anticipated, nor did I believe it was yet over. I had become a sore spot for some city council members who became increasingly hostile to my work on behalf of women. But I was not totally without support. Among elected officials, I had the backing of the mayor, the city controller, and, later, the only African American city council member.

In the end, the dollar-a-year episode backfired on the council members. Many women identified with my being told that my work was of very little value. An organization quickly formed called the Advocates for the Women's Advocate. They met the evening following the "dollar-a-year" council meeting to plan strategies in support of the Women's Advocate.

The tremendous support I received after such an unnerving experience was very rewarding. Many of these supporters did not know me; their commitment was to the Office of Women's Advocate and what it meant for the many women who were now willing to fight on behalf of it. At the same time, I began to recognize that the issue was not a personal one for the council members. I was merely a symbolic figure, their efforts meant to keep women in their place. But they were catching a lot of heat for their efforts!

The following week when the council was again open to the public, over one hundred citizens, mostly women, showed up to speak for or against the Office of the Women's Advocate. This time I was in the audience, wanting to be directly aware of what took place. I also imagined that the action they had taken on my salary was considerably easier because they hadn't had to look me in the face. I was wrong. After the speakers had their say, the council immediately voted to abolish the position of Women's Advocate and, using their power over the budget, directed the mayor to draw up an ordinance to that effect. They could not actually fire me because I worked for the mayor, however, my position was a line-item in the budget, and they had the budgetary powers to strike it. The final vote was to be held the following week.

During that week, Women's Advocate supporters continued to pressure the city council. Another large press conference was held featuring Susan MacManus, a University of Houston professor in the department of political science. In her role as a consultant to the city's legal department, Dr. MacManus stated that the city was in violation of its commitment to affirmation action by its recent attack on the Office of Women's Advocate. Word spread that the ACLU was seriously considering a lawsuit for "infringement of Van Hightower's civil liberties." The threat of a lawsuit caused some confusion and nervousness on the part of the city council. At the suggestion of the mayor, I continued with my activities as the Women's Advocate.

The evening before the final vote by the council, an estimated six hundred advocate supporters held a candlelight vigil outside city hall. Some stayed all night. There was another rally just before the meeting. It was all to no avail. The council took their final action to abolish the Office of Women's Advocate.

Following the council's action, I walked out along with many supporters and a huge group of media representatives. While I was being interviewed outside the council chambers, the mayor made an announcement that he had just hired me as an affirmative action specialist to perform the same duties as that of the now-abolished Office of Women's Advocate. The mayor was able to use this budget maneuver because there were many affirmative action specialists in the budget, so if they still wanted to fire me, the council would have to fire all of them. To no one's surprise, most of the council members were furious.

As Judith Hendricks put it in her master's thesis, "This whole scenario received national coverage." The story was picked up by the wire services with articles appearing in the *New York Times, Mother Jones,* and the *Los Angeles Times.* Almost four thousand newspaper articles covered my story over the next decade or so, with print coverage ranging from Texas cities of Austin, Brownsville,

Long-time friend Dr. Susan MacManus (left) and Nikki (right).

Dallas, Del Rio, Galveston, Houston, Kerrville, Longview, Marshall, McAllen, Odessa, and San Antonio, to cities in other states, including Tucson, Arizona; Ithaca, New York; Green Bay, Wisconsin; Pocatello, Idaho; Burlington, North Carolina; Danville, Virginia; Bridgewater, New Jersey; Clovis, New Mexico; Lincoln, Nebraska; Honolulu, Hawaii; Minneapolis, Minnesota; and Cheyenne, Wyoming.

Hendricks further wrote that "Van Hightower received mountains of messages of support, including telegrams from Texas Congresswoman Barbara Jordan, former New York Congresswoman Bella Abzug," and many others. "Local newspapers were deluged with letters to the editor pro and con the Office, the issues, and Van Hightower herself. She appeared on numerous television and radio programs." I was acknowledged for my work on behalf of women in national magazines, such as the *Ladies' Home Journal* and *Redbook*.

After all the notoriety, my work life did change dramatically. I had always received a considerable amount of media attention, but after the battle with the city council, it became overwhelming. Phone calls, messages, interviews, and invitations to speak poured in. It was hard to believe the volume of people who contacted me after reading about my experience. Fortunately, I had people who volunteered in my office and at least one student intern to handle all the calls.

I assumed that the worst was over and that I could finally refocus my attention on creating services that women desperately needed. Women in the community now had high expectations that I would bring about change. I received calls from women who were being abused, women who had been sexually assaulted, women who had been sexually harassed on the job, married women who couldn't get credit in their names, women who needed referrals to doctors and lawyers. Calls also came from family members who were deeply concerned about their loved ones.

I tried to organize a referral system, but the fact was there were few services for women. For a battered woman, finding a place of safety, a place where the batterer could not find her, was close to impossible. I started checking with shelter services in the city, but they were almost all for men. The YWCA had had housing for women in the past, but at some point it closed. It was not entirely unusual for me to receive calls from men looking for shelter—I

NASA National Aeronautics and Space Administration

Lyndon B. Johnson Space Cente Houston. Texas 77058

Speaking to women employees at NASA.

could place a man within an hour. But I spent days looking for a place for a woman. In those moments I always remembered the council member who announced to the city, "Women don't need an advocate any more than men."

Regardless of the insensitivity of the all-male city council, other individuals and organizations in the Houston community tried to mobilize services for women. Any time I heard about one of these efforts, I contacted a representative to learn about what they were doing. Often this at least gave me a referral when I received some heartbreaking call. Even if the organization didn't have much to offer, they almost always had someone with more knowledge about the problem than I did.

Confronting the issue of violence against women, for example, was new territory for me. While I grew up in a violent home and had been threatened with sexual abuse, including rape, other than demanding that law enforcement improve their services and attitudes, I didn't at first see what role the feminist community could or should take. Once again, as my consciousness increased, I realized that violence against women was closely tied to economic stability and opportunity, or the lack thereof. It would be impossible to solve the problem of violence without solving the other problem: male economic power over women. If women were in fear or had no support services available to them, they were significantly weakened in their options in life.

Several faculty members at the University of Texas School of Public Health were taking a serious interest in the issue of violence against women. One professor, David Martin, got in touch with me to see if we could work together. I met with him and some of the other concerned faculty to share my knowledge of the efforts that were then underway. We decided that representatives of all the active groups should meet. When I called around I found that there was great interest.

A meeting held at the UT School of Public Health included representatives from the YWCA, which was working to create a shelter for battered women and children; a small rape crisis organization; a group called Women in Action, which was linked to Catholic Charities; the WRCC, which was in the process of forming a wide-ranging information and referral service; and several other groups as well as individuals. We all shared information about the projects we were working on, none of which had yet gotten very far off the ground, mainly due to lack of money. We held a couple more meetings before we reached the conclusion that the most efficient action would be to combine our efforts, creating a women's center that would link all of the various groups' services, projects, and activities. We called it the Houston Area Women's Center, and it would assume responsibility for raising funds and providing structural and administrative services.

Meanwhile, the Office of Women's Advocate continued to buzz with activity in spite of the city council. When Judith Hendricks decided to write her master's thesis on the office, part of her research would involve interviewing the mayor and city council members to seek their opinions about the advocate. She received some interesting responses:

One of the Councilmen informed me that my subject did not interest him and that he did not "Intend to give *that woman* any more publicity." Another's secretary told me that he wanted the issue to go away and would probably just procrastinate past my data collection deadline. One departed for Europe . . .

My experience with Councilman Mann was a peak experience. When convinced that I did not really wish to discuss "sopping with biscuits" and Kentucky Moonshine (which comments I can only guess were meant to establish his credentials as a "good Ole Boy"), he told me that Councilman Louis Macey would answer my questions for him and then took me to visit with the secretaries. There he drew two secretaries from their seats to display their figures, told me that the slimmer one was his favorite, that the other one had gotten fat when she gave up cigarettes, and bestowed a kiss on the embarrassed "favorite." He said that he guessed Van Hightower would consider him a "Male Chauvinist Pig." His comments on the attempts of "Lesbiums" to seduce file clerks strained credibility.

Another Councilman . . . told me that women should not be made more independent which would certainly happen if the Advocate had her way, and the Equal Rights Amendment was ratified. He stated that we are not ready for women who are raising little children to have "to hustle" for themselves.

The whole affair was eye-opening to me. I had no doubt that the mayor was supportive of the Office of the Women's Advocate. He was young and liberal and he understood the issues, yet he was a politician and could go only so far with his support. Most of the council members were something else again. Their behaviors proved that they were truly misogynistic. They did not hesitate to claim that they loved women, loved their wives, daughters, and so forth. I did not doubt that they did in their own limited way, but those relationships were very likely based on certain restrictions of behavior and deference to men. They did not grasp what the women's movement was about or what women wanted.

The fledgling Houston Area Women's Center managed to open a small shelter for battered women, money was coming in, and, on the whole, the work of the Women's Advocate was going well. Then came another blow: Mayor Hofheinz announced that he would not run for another term in November 1977. Nothing was said to me by any of the candidates who emerged to replace him, and no comments were made in campaign speeches about the future of the Office of the Women's Advocate. One of the people running was Council Member Macey, who had taken the lead on abolishing the Office of the Women's Advocate. Not a good sign.

The person elected in a runoff with Council Member Macey was a former councilman, Jim McConn, who had a long career in home building and development in Houston.

Shortly after McConn was sworn in as mayor, I made an appointment to visit with him. I took a pile of documents explaining my accomplishments and the awards I had received for my work. I told him about the plans for the Houston Area Women's Center and described how badly it was needed in Houston. The new mayor was very friendly and encouraging. He said he believed we could work together and that the work of the Office of Women's Advocate was important. He said he would like to look over the material I had brought and give it some thought, perhaps making small changes in the job description.

Farewell to Mayor Fred Hofheinz (left).

The afternoon of the following day, I was once again visited by a very large group of media with their cameras. Their message this time was that the mayor had just given the keynote address at the noon luncheon of the all-male Downtown Rotary Club, announcing that he was firing the Women's Advocate. I was told that the announcement received a great deal of applause. I waited in my office to receive the call I expected from the mayor telling me that I had been fired. It never came, so I took the initiative. He was not available until after office hours, so at 5:00 p.m., I was seated in his waiting area.

When he invited me into his office, I took a seat and got right to it. "We talked just yesterday," I pointed out. "You seemed very positive. What happened?"

"Oh," he said, "I am so embarrassed. I just got carried away with my speech and it seemed like a good time to make the announcement."

"You felt no need to talk to me first?" I asked.

"Oh, I really should have. It was just a mistake. Look, there is no rush to do anything. Take what time you need."

I got up. "Okay, thanks," I said, and left.

Some of his comments reported in the media included the following:

"He said he didn't want a women's advocate, 'because as mayor, I'm the advocate for all citizens.'"

"McConn, who announced his decision at a Rotary Club luncheon, said 'One or more of my administrative aides will be a woman,' but added that Ms. Van Hightower 'will not be a part of the McConn administration.'"

"'I just figured that this administration could do well without Nikki Van Hightower,' he said."

"'Ms. Van Hightower will be removed from the payroll of his staff after the next pay period,' McConn said."

I continued working. My attitude was that if he was going to get rid of me, he, or someone, was going to have to come to my office and tell me to leave. It was rather astonishing to me that no one came. I got the sense that he was afraid to talk to me. I understood that the council members made regular inquiries about my fate, but still nothing happened. I carried on for several weeks until I was offered a position as a radio talk show host with a local talk radio station, KTRH.

It had been quite a ride. I was the Women's Advocate for almost two years, had my salary reduced to $1 a year, and been fired twice, yet I was still there. I had a long list of things I had managed to change or attempted to change for women at city hall and was making significant progress in developing services for women in the community. In addition to the many speeches I gave and interviews I conducted, I hosted "The Women's Advocate's Hour" on KTRH Radio, providing me the opportunity to speak directly to women and men about the effects of inequality on their lives.

I took some satisfaction that McConn was defeated in 1981 after his second term by Kathy Whitmire, the city controller and first woman ever elected to Houston government.

5 International Women's Year

While I was fighting the battle for the rights of women in Houston, similar struggles were taking place both nationally and internationally. In 1967, the United Nations adopted the Declaration on the Elimination of Discrimination against Women, which stated that discrimination was "an offence against human dignity." It called on member states to abolish existing laws, customs, regulations, and practices that promoted and supported discrimination against women. Following the declaration, the UN set in motion plans for International Women's Year (IWY) with a conference to be held in Mexico City in 1975. The goal for the Mexico City conference was to have all member nations send representatives who would address worldwide discrimination against women.

It turned out to be something quite different than expected. The representatives at the formal conference were primarily government officials—27 percent men and 73 percent women. Those delegates, which numbered about a thousand, were obligated to represent the interests of their respective governments and, specifically, what those governments determined to be in the best interests of their female citizens. But when word of the conference spread, interest grew among non-governmental organizations as well as individuals, who made their way to Mexico City from countries around the world. There were approximately six thousand of these non-governmental participants, who truly were advocates for women.

When the UN learned about this massive number of unexpected visitors, they located a meeting of the non-governmental group on the opposite side of the city, probably to offset any possible conflict with the governmental representatives. The non-governmental group focused on the needs of ordinary women and was considerably more diverse than the formal conference delegates. Given the number of non-governmental participants, it was not possible to ignore them. Both groups were ultimately effective in cooperating and sharing communication. As a result, they put out an impressive body of policy recommendations.

The success of the Mexico City conference led to the UN extending International Women's Year, designating 1975 to 1985 as the UN Decade for Women, with plans for a series of international conferences. The second world conference would be held in Copenhagen in 1980; each member state would hold an IWY conference to gather information and prepare for it. The US conference was authorized and funded by Congress with a $5 million federal grant. In the history of the country, there had never been anything like this kind of federal involvement in support of women. The federal attention and funding lent the conference credibility and attracted the attention of women leaders throughout the country.

Houston was chosen as the site for the US National Women's Conference. According to the Texas State Historical Association's *Handbook of Texas,* "Houston had received national attention in 1976 when Mayor Fred Hofheinz named Nikki Van Hightower as the Houston Women's Advocate, one of the first such positions in the country. This appointment strongly influenced the National Commission on the Observance of International Women's Year to select Houston as its meeting site, although by the time of the conference Van Hightower's position had been eliminated by the City Council and she had moved to the mayor's office to continue her work."

Mayor Hofheinz selected me to be the city's liaison for conference planning, a position that had me actively tracking all the major planning groups. Approximately two thousand delegates from fifty states and six territories attended the conference, with an additional fifteen to twenty thousand non-delegates who came to participate and observe. Although the conference would bring a significant amount of money and favorable publicity to the city, there were still people who were negative about the whole idea. A Harris County Republican Party official noted that the conference was bringing "a gaggle of outcasts, misfits, and rejects" to Houston.

In advance of the Houston conference, each of the fifty states and six territories held their own local conferences to elect delegates to the national meeting and vote on the policy recommendations that would remove the barriers "to the full and equal participation of women in the life of our nation." The state and territorial meetings were open to all women over the age of sixteen. In the summer of 1977, more than 150,000 people participated in all states and territories. The Texas state conference, held in Austin, drew 2,600 women, who elected fifty-eight delegates to the Houston convention.

Regardless of my appointed role in coordinating the planning groups, I still had to submit my name to be considered as a delegate

The Houston delegates, silhouetted against a flattened world map, are, from left, Hortense Dixon, Marie Oser, Sharon Macha, Penny Brown, Sylvia Garcia, Nikki Van Hightower and Pokey Anderson. Three not pictured are Melva Becnel, Mary Castillo and Josephine Stewart.

Meet the Houston delegates

DIVERSITY IS what the National Women's Conference planners said they wanted in the state delegates, and they have it in the Houston contingent.

When the Texas Women's Meeting convened in Austin in June, participants elected 58 delegates and 10 of those are from Houston. The city has the largest bloc of votes in the state delegation, followed by Austin with nine.

Some of the Houstonians are married, some single and some divorced. There's an executive, a temporary secretary, a law student and homemakers.

Some are politically active, some are particularly interested and active in child care and more than one speaks out for the rights of lesbians.

They range in age from the 20s to the 50s. Meet the Houston delegates:

Pokey Anderson: 28 years old, single, temporary secretary, national co-chairman of the board of National Gay Task Force. She started a Houston Gay Political Caucus two years ago and actively sought nomination as a voice for lesbians.

Melva Becnel: 37, divorced, one child, primarily in the real estate business and a lawyer. She's a native Houstonian and has been active in the YWCA, the Travelers Aid and

the Black Organization for Leadership Development. She says she does not represent any particular group.

Penny Brown: 31, divorced, one child, a lawyer currently unemployed. She was on the law school faculty at the University of

(See HOUSTON, Page 7)

Houston-area delegates to the IWY National Conference in Houston, 1977. Courtesy of the Houston Chronicle.

to the Houston conference. My ego would have taken quite a hit had I not been elected, but, to my delight, I was.

Major policy issues had been identified at the Mexico City IWY conference. Referred to as the "core agenda," it included arts and humanities, battered women, childcare, credit, education, elective and appointive offices, employment, the Equal Rights Amendment, health, homemakers, international interdependence, media, offenders, older women, rape, and reproductive freedom. Each topic was discussed, amended, and voted on at the state and territorial conferences. A sincere effort was made to encourage genuine diversity among the attendees to the state conventions so that diversity would be continued at the Houston national convention. The federal legislation that established the conventions required variation in the economic, racial, ethnic, religious, and age characteristics of the attendees. It was no small effort to make the necessary contacts within each state and territory to accomplish this goal. The biggest challenge was attracting women from low socio-economic backgrounds and members of racial or ethnic groups who typically had not been recognized for their support of women's rights activities.

Needless to say, with such a diverse group came differing opinions and lively discussions on each of the core agenda issues. Delegates voted on every recommendation, and each needed a majority vote to be considered at the national conference. Reaching an agreement was not easy. Although many women knew each other, or knew of each other, the majority did not. It was a real challenge for all of us to cross the boundaries that usually defined our lives in order to build trust and reach agreement on our recommendations. The opportunity to learn and appreciate the perspectives of women from widely different backgrounds was tremendously educational for us all. The well-known and respected state conference leaders had the patience and skills to keep proceedings moving steadily forward. Awanah P. Anderson, a Native American woman from Wichita Falls and Irma Rangel from Kingsville led the Texas conference. Other leaders included Ann Richards, Sarah Weddington, Eddie Bernice Johnson, Ernestine Glossbrenner, and Marta Cotera. Most of them were officeholders in Texas.

Much discussion focused on ideological divisions that seemed impossible to bridge between those who supported movement toward equality between the sexes and those who resisted that change. The issues that created the most conflict were abortion, homosexuality, and the ERA. Ironically, Texas was one of the first states to ratify the federal Equal Rights Amendment and to amend its state constitution to include its own version of the ERA, both in 1972, though the changes did not come without a long, hard battle.

The International Women's Year National Women's Conference in Houston, the first national conference of women since the Seneca Falls Convention in 1848, which had no governmental funding, convened on November 18 and adjourned on November 21, 1977. By the time the convention got underway, Jimmy Carter was president of the United States. Carter was an enthusiastic supporter of the conference, as had been President Gerald Ford before him. To honor the legacy of the Seneca Falls Convention, a torch was lit in Seneca Falls, New York, and carried 2,610 miles to the Albert Thomas Convention Center in Houston by more than 2,000 women runners. In the last thrilling mile, three young Houston athletes

Nikki (at far right) speaking at the welcome rally for the IWY Conference delegates and the runners who had participated in the pre-conference run from Seneca Falls to Houston, with Congresswoman Bella Abzug (second from right). Courtesy of the Houston Area Women's Center.

carried the torch, flanked by feminist leaders Bella Abzug, Betty Friedan, and Billie Jean King, with hundreds of runners following to express their support of the conference.

The first plenary session began on Saturday, November 19. Approximately 2,000 delegates filled the floor of the convention center. The other 15,000 to 20,000 people lined up outside at dawn and waited patiently for their non-delegate tickets for seats in the stands. It was the most amazing gathering I've ever been involved in. When I entered the convention center and headed toward the Texas delegation, I felt like I was a new US senator entering the Senate chambers for the first time. I was not alone—all the women I talked with said entering the convention for the first time was a breathtaking moment.

On the dais was Fred Hofheinz, the mayor of Houston; Congress-woman Barbara Jordan; Bella Abzug, who had been appointed presiding officer of the convention by President Carter; three First Ladies—Rosalynn Carter, Betty Ford, and Lady Bird Johnson—as well as Coretta Scott King; Liz Carpenter; and Maya Angelou.

On the other side of Houston, a meeting took place of approximately thirty organizations known as the "pro-life, pro-family" coalition, which was led by Phyllis Schlafly. Even though vastly outnumbered on the issues, they attacked the convention delegates for supporting lesbian rights, legal abortion, and the Equal Rights Amendment.

During the convention, I had the great opportunity to meet and get to know many influential women, some more open and engaging than others. They all took an interest in the work we were doing at the local level in Houston, particularly the plans for a full-service women's center. I had received letters from many of them when I was the Women's Advocate in support of me during my conflict with the Houston City Council. After the conference ended, I felt comfortable contacting most of these women to ask for guidance and various kinds of support.

Among them were Mary Anne Krupsak, lieutenant governor of New York; Eleanor Smeal, a major force in the modern feminist movement and president and cofounder of the Feminist Majority Foundation; and Barbara Jordan, the first African American elected to the Texas Senate since Reconstruction and the first African

Pro-plan and ERA, or the Equal Rights Amendment, supporters attend the National Women's Conference. Courtesy of Sam C. Pierson Jr. and the Houston Chronicle. Image available on the Internet and included in accordance with Title 17 U.S.C. Section 107

*An exciting moment! Winning the vote for passage of the ERA resolution at the IWY Conference, November 20, 1977. Sylvia Garcia (*in front*) and Nikki (*in back*). Courtesy of the* Houston Chronicle.

American woman from the South elected to the US House of Representatives (for Texas's 18th District).

Particularly receptive were journalist Liz Carpenter, former aide to President Lyndon Johnson and press secretary to Lady Bird Johnson; Ann Richards, Democratic Party leader who was elected Texas state treasurer and went on to be elected governor in

A serious moment at the IWY Conference. Ann Richards (right), who would go on to become the 45th governor of Texas, and Nikki (left) among the Texas delegates.

1991; Frances "Sissy" Farenthold, a feminist, attorney, and political activist who served in 1968 as the only woman in the Texas House of Representatives; and Gloria Steinem.

One of the most famous women at the time, Steinem was a writer, lecturer, feminist organizer and activist, and cofounder of *Ms.* magazine. We'd had numerous mutual engagements over the years, and she was always kind, friendly, and interested in the work I was doing. I hold a great deal of admiration for her. She truly devoted her life to women's rights, both at the national and international levels.

Someone who tended to be rather testy whenever I encountered her was Betty Friedan, author of the blockbuster book *The Feminine Mystique* and cofounder and first president of NOW. I met her for the first time on the dais when the runners arrived at the convention center in Houston. As we stood beside each other we started talking about the issue of gay women and their role in the women's movement. She took the position that the rights of gay women did not fit in with the women's movement and would undermine the struggle of women's rights; she maintained that they should have their own separate movement. I took the position that gay women had been loyal supporters of the broader women's rights movement and that they looked to the movement to stand up for their rights and took pride in their participation. It was a tense discussion. I felt uncomfortable disagreeing with someone who was an early leader of the women's movement and whom I had always greatly admired for her vision and courage.

The next time I saw her was again in Houston, where she had been invited to speak to a local organization, not one with which I was involved. I wasn't aware of the event until I received a phone call from one of the organizers, who told me that Friedan had requested that I introduce her before she spoke. I was flattered to be asked and accepted immediately. I was particularly pleased for a couple of reasons: One, she was Betty Friedan! Two, it meant that our rather unpleasant exchange at the IWY Conference in Houston had been put aside. Frankly, I was surprised that she remembered me. That pleased me as well.

When I arrived at the reception before the event, I was directed to a table where Friedan was seated with several other people. I went over and introduced myself, but she did not seem to recognize me. I explained that, as she had requested, I would be introducing her. "Oh," she said with a lack of expression, "they asked me who I would like to have introduce me. I told them I didn't really know anyone in Texas except that Hightower person. They said that would be perfect and would try to make arrangements. Of course, who I meant was Jim Hightower." I was put off balance to say the least. "Doesn't he live here?" she asked. I said I thought he lived in Austin. Everyone at her table looked miserably embarrassed except Friedan. By this time, I was finding it pretty amusing. I laughed and told her I regretted the mistake but would do my best. I was not invited to join her table, so I just wandered off with the person I came with. One of the representatives from the organization followed me, apologizing profusely for the mistake. I assured her that I found it amusing and that she should not be concerned. I wrote it off as a funny mistake, good for speeches and writing.

I had put a lot of thought into the introduction. I summarized her background and expressed my admiration for the positive influence she had had on women everywhere, including me. When she got up to speak, she did not acknowledge me or anything I had said. My friend who accompanied me was fit to be tied. She gave a great speech. We left as soon as it was over. I am still amused by it.

The second plenary session of the IWY National Women's Conference convened on the afternoon of Saturday, November 19. One of the standout speakers was Jill Ruckelshaus, who had been a delegate to the IWY Mexico City conference, had served as head of the White House Office of Women's Programs, and was one of the founders of the National Women's Political Caucus. She told us, "By a recent Gallup Poll, 63 percent of all of the people in this country, male and female, young and old, support the goals of the women's movement. Yet the press and many politicians claim that women cannot agree on what they want. Why is total unanimity suddenly demanded on women's issues?"

Ruckelshaus also famously wrote one of the strongest calls to all feminists:

We are in for a very, very long haul . . . We are asking for everything you have to give. We will never give up . . . You will lose your youth, your sleep, your patience, your sense of humor, and occasionally . . . the understanding and support of people that you love very much. In return, we have nothing to offer you but your pride in being a woman and all your dreams you've ever had for our daughters, and nieces, and granddaughters . . . Your future and the certain knowledge that at the end of your days you will be able to look back and say that once in your life you gave everything you had for justice.

The purpose of the Houston IWY National Women's Conference was to write a Plan of Action that originated among and was endorsed by a broad representation of women. That was accomplished by the passage of resolutions on twenty-six major topics including: the ERA, abortion, lesbian rights, childcare, minority women, home-makers, battered women, education, rape, and health. The National Plan of Action was then submitted to Congress and to President Ford to be acted upon.

Unfortunately, the momentum faded when the conference ended. Even though the Senate granted a three-year extension for passage of the ERA (from 1979 to 1982), it still fell three states short of ratification—a crushing blow to most of us.

Although the policy outcomes at the federal level were disappointing, the overall impact of the International Women's Year on women's rights and the women's movement was extraordinarily successful. The IWY state and national conferences infused the women's movement with new energy and determination. The conference was held in 1977, long before the days of cell phones, the internet, and other technologies that provided instant communication. This gathering was the first opportunity for most of us to meet and talk to leaders of the women's rights movement, leaders of other national organizations that played a role in women's rights, and many other ordinary women who, like me, were struggling for the rights of women at the local level. Being a part of this mixture of people from across the country brought credibility to our causes. Vital publications about women and the women's movement were generated, such as *The Spirit of Houston*; new research on women's issues flourished; and the support of presidents, first ladies, elected officials, and the United Nations gave legitimacy to our efforts. Instead of being the brunt of jokes for our struggles to gain equality and services, we were, for the first time in history, center stage in the political arena. It didn't last long, but I truly believe it made a difference.

International Women's Year broadened our outlook, both nationally and internationally. Conferences in other countries (Mexico City in 1975, Copenhagen in 1980, Nairobi in 1985, Beijing in 1995) gave us opportunities to learn not only of our common concerns, such as education, health care, and violence, but also of the needs and concerns that were experienced in other countries but only indirectly affected women in the United States. Women in South American countries, for example, needed help with tree removal from ancestral lands, bilingual education, and clean water.

The Houston conference had a wonderful confidence-building and energizing effect on those of us who were fortunate enough to attend, and especially we who lived in Houston. The conferences made us address our own misunderstandings and lack of trust due to differences in race, religion, ethnicity, social class, and sexual orientation. We were effectively forced out of our comfort zones, creating a much stronger and diverse movement as a result. Although the ERA was not ratified, a wide array of federal and state legislation was passed addressing equal employment, credit, fair pay, violence against women, and equal educational opportunities. In Houston, we charged ahead with forming the Houston Area Women's Center, which provided services for sexual assault survivors, those who suffered from abuse in the home, and other women who needed support and assistance. The organization now serves thousands of women and their children each year and has the widespread respect of civic leaders and the public.

I and many others came away from the Houston IWY conference more knowledgeable and more invigorated to carry on our efforts toward equality. We found ourselves working in a much more positive environment. Women started gaining better electoral representation. Just among the Texas delegates, several women soon ran for office for the first time, and those who already held elected positions ran for higher office.

Sylvia Garcia became Houston city controller in 1980 and was elected to the Harris County Commissioners Court in 2002, then the Texas State Senate in 2013. She was elected to the US House of Representatives for the 29th District of Texas in 2018.

Eddie Bernice Johnson, who had been a Texas state representative since 1972, became a representative in the US Congress in 1993, representing the 30th District of Texas.

Ann Richards, who sat on the Travis County Commissioners Court in 1976, was elected Texas state treasurer in 1983, and governor in 1991.

And I ran and was elected Harris County treasurer in 1986.

I was forever changed, and the nation was forever changed by the 1977 International Women's Year National Conference in Houston. Maya Angelou said it all in her moving speech published in the official report of the conference, *The Spirit of Houston*, which she titled "To Form A More Perfect Union":

> *We American women view our history with equanimity.*
> *We allow the positive achievement to inspire us and*
> *the negative omissions to teach us.*
> *We recognize the accomplishments of our sisters, those*

*famous and hallowed women of history and those
unknown and unsung women whose strength gave
birth to our strength.*

*We recognize those women who were and are immobilized
by oppression and crippled by prejudice.*

*We recognize that no nation can boast of balance until
each member of that nation is equally employed and
equally rewarded. We recognize that women collec-
tively have been unfairly treated and dis-honorably
portrayed.*

*We recognize our responsibility to work toward the
eradication of negatives in our society and by so
doing, bring honor to our gender, to our species, and
to ourselves individually.*

*Because of the recognition set down above we American
women unfold our future today.*

*We promise to accept nothing less than justice for every
woman.*

*We pledge to work unsparingly to bring fair play to every
public arena, to encourage honorable behavior in each
private home.*

*We promise to develop courage that we may learn from
our colleagues and patience that we may attack our
opponent.*

Because we are women, we make these promises.

Maya Angelou, 1977

Each successive international women's conference set a different
goal. The goal of the 1975 Mexico City conference was to establish
a World Plan of Action for the advancement of women's rights.
Mid-decade conferences were held individually by each member
country, including the one held in Houston in 1977. Each country,
totaling 145, completed a review of their own issues related to
women's rights and measured them against the Mexico City goals.

The purpose of the Second World Conference on Women, held
in Copenhagen in 1980, was to recognize the signs of the disparity
of rights between men and women. The conference representatives

unanimously agreed on three things that were essential for equality: equal access to education, equal employment opportunity, and adequate health care services.

The Third World Conference on Women was held in Nairobi in 1985, with 1,900 delegates from 157 member states represented at the public conference. Truly remarkable were the 12,000 people associated with non-governmental organizations (NGOs) or who were there as individuals. The goal of the Nairobi conference was to review and appraise the achievements of the UN Decade for Women and to develop forward-looking strategies. Included in those strategies were the promotion of equality at the national level and the promotion of women's participation in peace and development efforts.

Women at that time not only had little input into international affairs, they had little input into national governance. The conferences forged a path for women's full participation in politics and government. Women were eager to assume those new roles, but, regardless of the policy issues that came out of the international conferences, women still had to face opposition in places of power.

In 1995, the Fourth World Conference on Women was held in Beijing, China. The public conference had 5,000 delegates representing individual countries and an astounding 31,000 individuals and representatives from NGOs. Because China had concerns about having so many women in one location, the individuals and NGOs were farmed out to Huairou, a forty-five minute (fifty-three kilometer) bus ride from Beijing. The difficulty of the trip to China gave evidence of the dedication of women around the world to break through the barriers to women's rights. There were visas to be arranged, travel plans, and expenses. In China, delegates had to contend with rainy days, deflated tents, stiflingly hot rooms, and massive numbers of security guards. Bella Abzug sized it up:

Imperfect though it may be, the Beijing Platform of Action is the strongest statement of consensus on women's equality, empowerment, and justice ever produced by governments . . . It is an agenda for change, fueled by the momentum of civil society, based on a transformational vision of a better world for all.

> We are bringing women into politics to change the nature of politics, to change the vision, to change the institutions. Women are not wedded to the policies of the past. We didn't craft them. They didn't let us.

Regardless of the obstacles, thousands of women made their way to the international conferences on their own. They caucused in groups and engaged in conversations, overcoming the language barriers. They visited with the local people who joined them out of curiosity. Vital information was shared and passed on to government-appointed delegates. As it turned out, the shared knowledge from the NGOs and individuals significantly enriched each conference.

A US delegate to the conference in Beijing, Maria Berriozábal, from San Antonio, gave her impression of their accomplishments in her book *Maria, Daughter of Immigrants*: "While the documents produced by the conference were good, they were not enforceable. What women were able to do with the information they gathered from each other and the networks they built, however, was incalculable."

One of the highlights of the Beijing conference was First Lady Hillary Clinton's speech to the plenary session. White House officials had discouraged her from going to the conference and making a speech due to the possibility of negative diplomatic fallout. She took things into her own hands and made a speech that still resonates twenty-three years later. Especially memorable was her statement, "If there is one message that echoes forth from this conference, let it be that human rights are women's rights and women's rights are human rights once and for all."

Most of us who participated in the UN women's conferences — international, national, and state — came away inspired by the experience, the research and materials that were developed afterward, and the education we received from our interactions. We also suffered disappointment from the failure of governments and the UN to follow through on the implementation of policies, but overall the conferences represented a highly positive achievement.

6 A Short Media Career

During the IWY National Women's Conference in Houston in November 1977, I remained in my position as the city's Women's Advocate, although it was no longer officially called that. After Mayor Fred Hofheinz's term ended on December 31, the incoming mayor, Jim McConn, fired me as one of his first actions in office in January 1978. But I didn't actually leave the position until March, when I accepted a position as a call-in talk show host for KTRH Radio in Houston. I already had a weekly show at KTRH called the "Women's Advocate's Hour," during which I typically answered questions about my work and women's rights.

The new show, called "Double Talk," was cohosted by Ed Brandon, who was also the weather person for a local television station and had hosted the show alone until I was hired to share the program with him. Needless to say, the partnership format changed the nature of the show. My presence attracted many calls concerning issues that were controversial: whether or not we should have a women's advocate, the women's movement and feminism, the ERA, and reproductive rights, plus some general objections to my presence on the show. After some time the subject matter began to broaden as we started receiving calls on more general topics. After about six months of working together, Ed left the show, and the calls turned hostile again, accusing me of driving Ed away. Ed had always been friendly and pleasant to work with, so I had no reason to think that I was the cause of his leaving. I missed him for one very practical reason—when there was a lull in phone calls, we could talk to each other until the calls picked up again. Whatever the reason for his departure, I was then on my own.

The work gave me a great respect for the power of the media. I have been amazed at how, years later, people have more memories of me from that radio show than from any of my other endeavors. Part of my responsibility at the station was to write daily opinion pieces; these were recorded and played twice a day. I focused my opinions mainly on issues related to human rights, including gender, race, homophobia, and current issues of the day. The opinion pieces also gave me an opportunity to discuss those subjects when I was on the air in the afternoons.

Occasionally I would have a guest. When Gloria Steinem was in town to speak at a function, I invited her to be on the show. She was delightful to interview. During one incoming call, the male caller rudely asked, "Are you a lesbian?" She responded immediately with the question, "Are you the alternative?" There was a broadcast delay on the station just for such circumstances, but her response was so quick and so clever that they opted not to black it out. I had tremendous admiration for her skill in handling verbal assaults.

Another memorable interview was with Madalyn Murray O'Hair, founder of American Atheists. She was quite a character. She arrived with three or four members of her family. They all had very loud voices and talked a mile a minute. She asked when we would be going on the air (in just twenty minutes) then said they wanted a beer and asked for the nearest place to get one. I pleaded with them not to be late! They weren't, but they came back with beer in hand, which was very likely their second round. They were even livelier than before.

O'Hair's purpose was to defend the civil rights of non-believers and fight for the separation of church and state. She published the early issues of *American Atheist Magazine* and brought two successful lawsuits (*Murray v. Curlett*, 1962 and 1963) to the Baltimore, Maryland, Court of Appeals, which handed down a decision banning Bible reading in public schools. In 1963, the US Supreme Court upheld the ruling in an eight-to-one decision in *Abington School District v. Schempp*.

In an interview with *Playboy Magazine* in 1965, she referred to herself as a militant feminist and offered some of her thoughts about men: "To him, sex appeal is directly proportional to the immensity of a woman's tits. I'm not saying that all American men are this way, but nine out of ten are breast-fixated, wham-bam-thank-you-ma'am cretins." Between the general hostility of the religious public to her cause and her unusual personality, she made a lot of enemies. Although I shared many of her thoughts on religion, she arrived at the radio station prepared for battle, anticipating nothing but hostility toward herself and her ideas. Most of the calls she received fit her expectations.

On the whole, I enjoyed the work on the radio. Although writing a daily opinion piece was demanding, the ensuing conversations gave me a tremendous amount of airtime, and people were listening. I couldn't help but appreciate the opportunity I had been given to share my ideas with a large segment of the population. I noticed that the hostility tapered off somewhat over time, and that people began to engage with me in more thoughtful discussions.

Categorizing people who are drawn to call-in talk shows was a habit of mine. This was an over-generalization, but in my mind they tended to fall into two groups. One was lonely people. I noticed that group particularly during or around holidays. I sensed that they were alone and felt like talking to someone. That group was comfortable carrying on conversations about ordinary life. They didn't have to be taking a position on an issue.

The other group was made up of angry people. They were mad at politicians, political policies, and me. They raged about my having been the Women's Advocate and about what they considered my liberal thinking. One thing that tended to get under their skin was my PhD. It was not unusual to be accused of lying about it. I really opened myself up to an attack from one caller: He asked me a question about numismatics, and when I foolishly admitted that I was not familiar with the word, he tore into me. "How can you have a PhD and not know what that word means? I knew what that was when I was in grade school!" and so on. He was so delighted to have caught me on my lack of knowledge that I didn't think I would ever get him off the phone. I explained to him that earning a PhD meant specializing in a particular area of knowledge, mainly for research purposes, but he would not hear it.

Ratings were always a hot topic around the station. One day after ratings had just been released, the sales manager stopped by to congratulate me on how well the show was doing. He told me it oscillated between second and fourth in a twenty-eight-station market. I couldn't help but feel pleased. After all, it was a free-wheeling show, such that I had a great deal of independence and control. Ironically, at around that same time the atmosphere around the station began to change. The two top managers were suddenly uncommunicative; when I passed them in the hall, they would glance away and not speak to me. I took their behavior to mean that my time was probably limited at KTRH Radio.

I was not surprised when the station manager and assistant manager finally arrived in my office. They looked so uncomfortable I almost felt sorry for them. The station manager told me he regretted having to do it, but he was going to have to let me go. "Why?" I inquired. With a straight face, he told me that the ratings for the show were just too poor. I am sure I couldn't keep a small a sneer from my face as I informed them that the sales manager had just told me the ratings for my show were very good and that he was pleased. It was obvious they did not expect me to have this information. After a few moments of uncomfortable silence, they responded, "Well . . . they are good, but just not good enough." I started to ask them what "good enough" might be, but I knew I would be wasting my time.

As I left, I stopped to say goodbye to people in the station who had, on the whole, been very supportive of me. One of the associate producers, Danette Comardo said, "It's no surprise. The [IWY] Conference and the equal rights movement, that's too hot of a talk show topic around here."

I had never considered hosting the radio show to be a long-term job, but this latest firing was rough on my life. It had been a very good arrangement. I came in an hour or so before I went on the air, earlier on the days when I had to record my opinion pieces. The rest of my time I spent working on the development of the women's center or giving talks. I still received a lot of speaking invitations. The radio salary was low, but livable.

I was beginning to wonder if I was so controversial that I was unemployable. The irony was that I was hired to do things that were, by their nature, controversial. When I was fired, it was because I was effective.

It was then March 1979, marking almost exactly one year that

I had been with the radio station. Shortly after I left I received a phone call from a representative of the National Commission on Working Women in Washington, DC. She explained that they had awarded me first place in their 1979 Women at Work Broadcast Awards for Radio/Television Editing. The woman began the conversation by telling me that she was very glad to get in touch with me. They wanted to present the award to me alongside all of the other award winners at their banquet in Washington, DC. The award would specifically recognize me for my daily opinion pieces that I wrote and broadcast for KTRH radio.

After I responded that I was truly honored to receive the award, she told me she had called KTRH Radio and explained the award, but the radio station told her they had no knowledge of how to get in touch with me, which was, of course, ridiculous. They knew exactly how to get in touch with me because the information was in their personnel files. She said that she suspected something was fishy, so she made a couple of calls, finding me in only a few minutes. I was shocked to hear of this singularly graceless act on the part of the KTRH station manager. I was looking forward to the trip to Washington, DC, to receive the award at the banquet, but unfortunately there was a family death at the same time, so a university friend of mine from NYU, Marilyn Falik, attended on my behalf.

I decided I was not going to ignore the station's pettiness, so I called the station manager, told him what I had just learned, and demanded an explanation. Of course, he had no explanation. He said he was sorry for the misunderstanding and offered me congratulations for the award. I told him that it was a low thing to do. Didn't he think the award was also an honor for the radio station? As I recall, the conversation quickly ended.

Approximately another year later, I received a call from this same station manager, who asked if we might have lunch. My curiosity got the best of me, so I said yes. Much to my surprise, his purpose for asking me to lunch was to give me an explanation and an apology. He told me that he, in fact, had not wanted to fire me and that he had been pleased with my show. He said that it had come down to either him losing his job or me losing mine. Of course, it was me. The driving force for the firing, according to him, was that the station owners did not like the show. They were very conservative people who felt there was too much emphasis on feminism. They wanted a more broad-based show.

Since I had no control over who called in and what they wanted to talk about, the only way to change the nature of the show was to change the host. I am not sure exactly what he hoped to gain from sharing this information with me. I assumed that he had hoped to unburden himself of some guilt. I told him I appreciated the explanation. That was where the matter, and my professional media career, ended.

Some of the best media coverage I received was from a local magazine called *Houston Breakthrough*. The magazine, which covered feminist issues and featured articles about women's lives and the women's movement, was cofounded by Janice Blue and Gabrielle Cosgriff, who shared the editing duties. It was published bimonthly from 1976 to 1980, and included coverage of the Office of Women's Advocate. For my work on the radio, I received two awards from the magazine: Woman of the Year Award in 1976 and *Houston Breakthrough* Media Award for Excellent Coverage of Women's News in 1977. In the final issue, the founders wrote a moving farewell letter to their loyal readers, stating: "We started *Breakthrough* to fill a need in the community and focused on feminist and progressive issues, areas that we felt have been sorely neglected by the local press."

Several articles in *Houston Breakthrough* held a particular meaning for me, such as the story of my appointment to the position of Women's Advocate in 1976. A special issue in 1977 covered my initial firing by the city council and a description of many of my accomplishments as Women's Advocate. Another article, entitled "Tribute to Nikki," in 1978 focused on a letter from Sally Chalmers, a supervisor at the Houston Zoo who had named a four-week-old spotted black leopard after me. Holding that baby leopard, whose mother was pacing just behind the cage shown in the photo, was an absolute joy for me.

I had the honor of being the cover story for another local publication, *Houston City* magazine, in April 1987, shortly after I took office as Harris County treasurer. To my regret, that was the last issue published. The author was Marion Knox Barthelme, who did

Letter of tribute from Sally Chalmers, a supervisor at Houston's Hermann Park Zoo.

CITY OF HOUSTON
INTER OFFICE CORRESPONDENCE

TO NIKKI VAN HIGHTOWER

FROM SALLY CHALMERS
SUPERVISOR: PRIMATES, CATS, BEARS
HERMANN PARK ZOO

DATE JAN. 23, 1978

SUBJECT A SPECIAL LEOPARD

DEAR MS. VAN HIGHTOWER,

ON DEC. 13, '77 THE HOUSTON ZOO HAD ITS FIRST BLACK LEOPARD BIRTHS EVER — ONE MALE AND ONE FEMALE. THE CUBS ARE HEALTHY AND BEAUTIFUL AND ARE BEING RAISED BY THEIR MOTHER. I THOUGHT YOU MIGHT BE INTERESTED IN THIS EVENT BECAUSE WE'VE NAMED THE FEMALE "NIKKI." SHE IS FEISTY BUT GENTLE AND OUTWEIGHS HER BROTHER, SO SHE SEEMED A PERFECT TRIBUTE TO YOU AND ALL YOU'VE DONE FOR WOMEN CITY EMPLOYEES. I MUST ADMIT THAT SOME OF THE MEN IN MY DEPART-MENT GRUMBLED OVER THE SELECTION OF THE NAME, BUT THEY TEND TO BE MACHO ANYWAY AND, LUCKILY, I OUTRANK THEM.

IF YOU'D LIKE TO SEE YOUR NAMESAKE UP CLOSE, PLEASE FEEL FREE TO LOOK ME UP OR CALL ME. MY OFFICE IS IN THE GORILLA HABITAT (5260850) AND I'M HERE SUNDAY THROUGH THURSDAY. I'D LOVE TO SHOW YOU AROUND.

SINCERELY,

Sally Chalmers

"Nikki," a four-week-old spotted leopard named after Nikki, the Women's Advocate. What a thrill!

THE TRUTH ABOUT TEXAS, PART I PAGE 6:

Houston City

APRIL 1987

$2 00

NIKKI!

Houston's first feminist
versus the good ol' boys

FIGHTING FOR LIFE

Inside the world's only
AIDS hospital

ROBERT MOSBACHER

Bush's buddy blends
Yankee know-how and
southern savvy

EXCITING SPRING FASHIONS:

The Houston Look

Nikki Van Hightower
Harris County Treasurer

Nikki on the cover of Houston City *magazine. Courtesy of* Houston City.

an extensive amount of research. I found her to be highly insightful.

"People see a certain amount of steel in the 47-year-old Van Hightower and that was probably tempered long ago. When she helped to launch the Houston Area Women's Center in 1977 for women in crisis, it didn't occur to her, consciously at least, that she had firsthand experience in an abusive family. 'It's funny that you can live in a home like the one I was raised in and not consider it violent because it's all you know.'"

Barthelme shared her thoughts on writing the article:

I sat down to a sheaf of newspaper clips from those days. I was mildly curious to learn about the women's movement in Houston, to discover what the Women's Advocate had done to cause such a stir. I felt detached as I began to read; this was simply research and very quaint, very passé. But as I continued, small stirrings in indignation began to form, and as I went on, I began to get really angry. What happened?

Van Hightower, I reasoned, had emerged from a background in which she had directly experienced women's disadvantages, either through meager resources, a bad marriage (her mother's and grandmother's), or a dearth of opportunity and education. She'd worked her way up out of a mingy lower-middle-class existence by sheer willpower and brains to a fairly high-level government job, whose main purpose was to promote and protect women. She's a solid citizen, a university professor, a rational but wised-up and judicious person. Not a firebrand. "I'll win over city council," she thought. "If I talk to them, they'll understand." But they didn't. They should have had Bella Abzug screaming at them as did their New York counterparts. Then they would have appreciated Van Hightower.

"She handled the job with great skill, politically and technically," remembers Hofheinz. "But the average time on city council of each member was over 10 years; some had been there for 25. It was the early days of affirmative action, the new thing that was happening in America. But Houston was behind America.

"She didn't let much slip by, either. There were many issues of substance; others, more token in nature, a good old girl might have ignored. She criticized city officials who boasted of being male chauvinist pigs. She chided two city department managers who complained that the behavior of some female employees was menopausal."

With the time freed up from my radio life, I devoted virtually all my energy to the development of the Houston Area Women's Center. It had become an official charitable organization, and the demands for crisis services were increasing rapidly. The necessity for more funds was growing at an equal pace, so I pushed relentlessly to raise money. As president of the board of directors and a founding member of the organization, I was determined that the Houston Area Women's Center was not going to fail.

7 Houston Area Women's Center

Establishing crisis services for women in Houston became the main focus of my work throughout 1977 and 1978. Initially the work was linked to the Office of the Women's Advocate, but as time went on, more groups and individuals became involved. In 1977 we made some major advances in the services we were able to offer and in setting up the Houston Area Women's Center as an official nonprofit organization.

Our association with the University of Texas School of Public Health in Houston was tremendously helpful. They provided free office and meeting space, communication services, skilled faculty members who could not have been more supportive of the program, and crucial credibility at this early time.

We applied to the Internal Revenue Service for a 501(c)(3) authorization, which would essentially qualify us as a charitable organization with nonprofit status. This meant that we would not be subject to income taxes and that donations to the center would be tax-deductible as charitable contributions. To qualify for this status, we had to state our objectives for serving the community and verify that we were an existing organization, which required us to have a president and a treasurer.

We selected a board of directors from people who were currently involved in the project and a few others who were recommended to us. I was selected to be the president of the board. We officially named the organization the Houston Area Women's Center (HAWC). It was a big step for us. We had no regular source of income and we couldn't raise much money until we were officially tax-exempt, which took a while. The issue of lack of diversity on the board immediately came up—there were too few women of color and not enough lesbian representation. There were also complaints that services such as alcohol and drug abuse recovery were not in the plans. We immediately added new people to the board, which grew to be very large. I interpreted some of the complaints as a tacit recognition that something important was getting ready to happen and so activists wanted to see that their interests were represented.

Once we received our nonprofit status, we were officially one organization. This might seem obvious and certainly no cause for any conflict. However, our new organization, HAWC, was made up of pre-existing groups who had already made inroads in getting their individual services off the ground: help for battered women, rape services, and information and referral services for women in need. They were operating only with volunteers, but each group had established its own identity; they were reluctant to abandon their individual identities to become an official part of the Houston Area Women's Center. These individual groups, particularly their leaders, wanted to be part of the women's center and receive the benefits of funding and other administrative support services, but they wanted to remain largely independent in their program operations.

I could foresee this disagreement taking us back to square one if we didn't find an acceptable compromise. The compromise we finally reached allowed the groups to maintain much of their independence in decision-making related to their delivery of services, but they would identify themselves as an HAWC program, be represented on the board, and have expenses and personnel matters (when there were any personnel) financially supported and approved by the board of directors. Some of the board members who were not directly tied to any individual service group were not particularly happy about this arrangement, but I was not one of them. I knew there was going to be a tremendous amount of work in fundraising and organization-building, much of which would fall to me, so I was satisfied with letting specific individuals continue the responsibility of operating the various services they had founded.

Beyond developing an organizational structure, the women's center took several big steps forward in 1977. The first crucial service that began operating as part of the women's center was the Women's Information, Referral, and Exchange Service (WIRES), originally founded by Women in Action, part of the Catholic

Charities of the Archdiocese of Galveston-Houston. They had built their program with the goal of eventually becoming part of a women's center, therefore they didn't suffer the same identity crisis as some of the other programs. WIRES became a crucial part of the women's center. It formed the hub in the wheel of our other programs because much of the communication for access to those programs flowed through WIRES. They brought with them a list of referrals that had already been vetted and were tremendously helpful. Their wonderfully experienced volunteers gladly moved their operations to our space in the UT School of Public Health. The leader of WIRES was a highly skilled volunteer by the name of Adelyn Bernstein. Besides handling crisis calls, WIRES collected valuable data on the needs of women and children in the Houston community. The only thing they were reluctant to do in terms of fully uniting with the women's center was to change their name from WIRES. The compromise we reached was that they would answer the phone by saying, "Women's Center—WIRES." All were satisfied.

The next important development was that a house was loaned to us for use as a shelter. When word spread that a shelter was available, the small three-bedroom house quickly filled with desperate women and their children. The question then became how to manage the shelter. The women's center had no paid staff; we relied completely on volunteers. Our volunteers responded by becoming even more generous with their time, but the dilemma of turning people away because there was no more space available remained. We established a policy of a maximum three-week stay. During that time, the women were expected to determine how to put their lives back together. It was not easy.

About this time, we found that we were able to take advantage of the federal Comprehensive Employment and Training Act (CETA). The act provided funds for hiring people for eighteen-month periods during which time they received a salary for their training and then for performing needed duties. Because the women's center had not yet received its nonprofit status, another organization that was sympathetic to our cause and qualified for CETA grants hired three people under their organization and loaned them to us. We placed one person at the new shelter to handle some management responsibilities and two at the women's center headquarters for administrative duties. As I write this, one of them, Janet Stewart, is still employed with the women's center and plans to stay there until she retires.

I will never forget the day Janet arrived for an interview. Originally from a rural area, she had worked in nursing before moving to Houston. We were looking for an administrative assistant—typing, answering the telephone, and keeping records. She was certainly qualified for those duties. As she was leaving, she turned back to us and said, "I really want to work for the Houston Area Women's Center." She completely won us over with her sweet personality and her sincere expression of commitment to the women's center. Janet's commitment was real—today she is one of the top administrators at HAWC. The three CETA employees were helpful but did not resolve our need for experienced program staff. Demands on the women's center were growing rapidly. After I was no longer employed with KTRH Radio, I assumed many of the responsibilities of a director, but at the same time I was unenthusiastically seeking other employment, as I needed income.

By 1979, both the organization and I were stretched thin. What little money we had raised was used for the cost of the shelter. The board of the women's center recognized the obvious and offered me the position of executive director. The position came with a salary, but it was up to me to raise it. By this time, we had received our nonprofit status, meaning that raising money quickly became my main priority. Because there was still considerable misunderstanding about violence against women, I focused first on foundations. Most were used to dealing with people's misery, and their leaders were generally open-minded. They were also interested in funding new and innovative programs. I had hoped to receive United Way funding; however, we learned that they did not support organizations until they had been in existence for at least three years. When they did provide funding, they restricted many types of supplemental fundraising, almost completely limiting organizations to fundraising events. To raise money in that manner, it was essential to have a board of directors that had relationships with other people who could be called upon to make sizeable contributions.

I was relentless with my fundraising, and soon it was paying off. We were able to purchase another building for the shelter near downtown Houston. It was an old building that had been remodeled as a shelter. Another organization's plans to purchase it had fallen through, but it was perfect for the women's center—at least for a time. Demands continued to grow. When the CETA employee at the shelter left, our funds were such that we were able to hire a director who had the necessary skills for the demanding job.

The one program the women's center had difficulty getting underway was service for survivors of sexual assault. The leader of the group with a small program resisted any direction from the women's center. She continued to be concerned that they would lose their identity as an independent program even though we had reached a compromise on this matter. The outcome was that part of her organization stayed at the women's center while the unhappy leader and a few others left. It meant restarting this essential service almost from scratch.

To have an effective rape (sexual assault) crisis service required meeting some heavy demands. There had to be a large enough number of volunteers to cover phone lines twenty-four hours a day, seven days a week. They needed to receive extensive training. Individual phone lines had to be installed. Either the volunteers came in to headquarters for their shifts or the calls had to be transferred to their home phone lines, which could be answered only by the volunteer. It was also important for other volunteers to be available to escort and assist the survivors as they made their way through the difficult and demeaning process of reporting the crime. It was a complicated and demanding program. We began to resolve these difficulties when I hired Adelyn Bernstein, the founder of WIRES, to be the director of the sexual assault program.

I first met Adelyn shortly after the 1977 IWY conference. During the conference, I had been interviewed about the idea of a women's center with a broad range of services. She picked up on that idea and, following the conference, organized a meeting of women leaders to talk about coordinating efforts for women's services. At that meeting she talked about starting an information and referral service for women that would eventually become part of a women's center. I must admit that I was a little dubious about her at first. She

Nikki (left) and Adelyn (right) on Adelyn's ninetieth birthday.

had not been active in the women's rights movement until then. She had devoted most of her adult life to valuable civic-minded projects, but I believed that the women's center should be more than crisis services for women. It had a political purpose, a mandate to bring about change in the status of women in relation to men. This was a feminist organization. I did not want us to lose our edge.

I completely underestimated Adelyn. She was a charming and dedicated person who brought many volunteers with her when the women's center and WIRES coalesced. She was a master at organizing volunteers. She treated them with a great deal of dignity but demanded discipline. She herself was organized, disciplined, and demanding. I had always been under the impression that you had to treat volunteers differently than staff, but Adelyn took volunteer work very seriously and she successfully passed her commitment on to the volunteers. WIRES was the one program we never had problems managing.

When WIRES was established at the women's center head-quarters, which was one large room in the UT School of Public Health, it was impossible not to overhear our side of the phone conversations and get a sense of the subjects being addressed. It did not take long before the WIRES volunteers became a hotbed of feminists. They listened during their shifts to the difficulties, abuse, and discrimination that women were enduring and it left them angry, even though they probably had no experience of such treatment themselves. One matter they took very personally. The federal Equal Credit Opportunity Act had been passed in 1975 and was amended in 1976. Even with twelve enforcing agencies, enforcement was still very lax, and there had not been adequate publicity of the act. While some women were finding it easier to obtain credit in their own names, the majority were not. The result of these inadequacies in enforcement was that many eligible people, particularly women, were denied protection of their access to credit. Many calls came in from women who were furious for having their credit cancelled after they married or for being denied credit after they were divorced or widowed. After referring many women to the proper enforcement agency for filing complaints, the volunteers, who felt quite certain that they had credit in their own names, began calling institutions where their families had credit, only to receive the unpleasant information that the credit was only in their husbands' names. Even when their own names were on their credit cards, they were not personally receiving the benefit of a record of credit. To add to the insult, most of these women held the major responsibility for their families' finances—managing income, budgeting, and paying bills. I listened to the volunteers express their anger at the credit issue and many other problems with which they began to identify. I realized I had no cause to be concerned about their commitment to feminism.

Adelyn was a wonderful leader of the WIRES program, but I had decided I needed someone with her skills for the rape crisis program. I anticipated that she would be hard to replace at WIRES, but, to my surprise, one of the WIRES volunteers, whose education and training was as an engineer, asked to be considered for the job as director. As we were required to do, we posted the job, but there were few applicants and no one with her experience, devotion to the program, and the support of Adelyn. She became the new director, loved the job, and was in turn loved by the volunteers. It was incredibly satisfying to watch these careers develop. Many years later the second director of WIRES moved to another part of the country, where she founded a women's information and referral system.

Adelyn began taking on the challenge of the rape program by educating herself on the subject. She visited with the few experts in the field, then constructed an extensive training program. We already had a few volunteers, and she set about recruiting more. Initially she took many of the shifts herself to become personally familiar with the experience of talking to survivors and learning about the kinds of skills necessary to handle the crisis line. The communication lines were set up. Hospital emergency rooms, schools, churches, and criminal justice agencies were notified, and we went to work. It became a wonderfully successful program.

Fundraising was my first priority. Thanks to help from foundations, I was reaching the point where I could sleep at night. My second priority was community education, which was closely linked to fundraising. My path to becoming executive director of the women's center came through my involvement in the women's rights movement and my experience as the Women's Advocate. My thinking was political, in the sense of working toward equal rights for women, as well as service-oriented. My work as the Women's Advocate forced me to come to terms with the deep connections between women's political rights and their safety and security. Violence against women, the absence of political power, the lack of services—these problems women faced were tied together, and the solutions all required money and policy changes.

When my status changed from the Women's Advocate to the head of the women's center, I sensed a mellowing of public attitude toward me. Caring for women in crisis was a more traditional role and was much more tolerated, by men at least, than overtly pressing for women's equality, which was considerably more threatening. I took advantage of that change in attitude by becoming heavily engaged in educating the public about violence against women.

Blaming the victim was a common way of thinking about violence against women: "women ask for it," "it doesn't really happen—they make it up," and "it doesn't happen to people like us." Part of the reason that these myths and misunderstandings were so resistant to change was that there was no reliable data on violent crimes against women. Unfortunately, that is still largely true today. In cases of domestic violence when law enforcement was called, which it often was not, it was common for officers not to bother to show up because domestic violence was not considered a "real" crime unless there was a death. Sometimes law enforcement came by, settled things down, and left without making a report or, if they did make a report, did not disclose the nature of the relationship. As a result, domestic violence was vastly underreported.

To this day, sexual violence against women remains seriously underreported. Women are reluctant to report such crimes for many reasons: personal embarrassment, thinking they will not be believed, feeling like they were somehow responsible, and the humiliation usually suffered during the reporting process. Often women know their attackers and were with them voluntarily. Such is the case with date rape. Also, they might have been drinking or partying.

Data gaps in crimes against women exist around the world, not just in the United States. This serious flaw in crime statistics has been recognized by the European Union and the United Nations. Inadequate data leads to failure to pass laws to address female security. Although the United States and individual states have made significant progress in this regard, years of mistreatment of women when they do seek help for these crimes have resulted in serious underreporting.

To overcome the first line of resistance—the idea that "women ask for it"—I relied on stories of actual incidents. With WIRES operating and the shelter open, we had a considerable amount of material with which to work. We told the real-life, heartbreaking stories of women who called for help or came to the shelter. They were afraid that either they or their children might be badly hurt or killed, concerned that no one would believe them, or terrified that they would lose their children or be unable to care for them. Fear and shame ruled their lives. "Why don't women just leave?" was a common question. For those who know little about the subject, it sounds like such a simple solution. But leaving is not easy. Women are at highest risk when they try or threaten to leave. That is the reason shelters are in very secure locations. The women usually have few, if any, resources. If they have a job, they will probably have to leave it because returning daily to a known location will often prove dangerous for them. Leaving is extraordinarily disruptive to the lives of children, who can also be at risk. Sometimes children don't want to leave. Before shelters opened and became obvious and overflowing sanctuaries for abused women, police departments often didn't bother with those cases because they either didn't consider them to be real criminal matters or believed them too dangerous for the officers to respond to—too dangerous for trained, armed officers, but not too dangerous for the woman and possibly her children.

The way the women's center was structured, I had few occasions to involve myself directly with domestic violence cases. However, one Sunday afternoon, Irvin and I went downtown for a boat show. We parked in an underground lot and walked through the tunnels to the display area. When we were leaving, a couple and a young girl were walking in front of us. The man was yelling at the woman. I don't mean speaking loudly, I mean yelling. They climbed the stairs to the street level and stopped. Rather than going directly to our car, we followed them to the surface. He was still yelling at the top of his lungs in Spanish, shaking with rage. The woman and young girl stood frozen, terror on both of their faces. Concerned that this was turning into a very dangerous situation, we stopped nearby, thinking our presence might embarrass him enough to regain control of himself. Just as we stopped, the mother and the girl started running as if their lives were at stake, which they very well might have been. He did not chase them, but kept yelling, even directing some of his tirade at us. We went back down the stairs to get our car, which was still in the underground parking lot.

We began driving around downtown Houston in the direction the mother and daughter had been running. Fortunately, it was Sunday and there was very little traffic. After about fifteen minutes we found them hiding in the doorway of a closed building. Irvin stayed in the car while I got out to talk to them about what was happening and find out if they wanted to go to the shelter. It was clear that the mother did not understand English, but the young girl, who was about ten or eleven, did. I talked to them for several minutes. They were both shaking. Tears were running down the mother's face. It was evident she had no idea what to do. The young girl interpreted for her mother. Finally, the girl took the mother by the hand and led her to our car. We drove them to our house, fed the girl (the mother would not eat), and called the shelter volunteer who was on duty. We still had no staff at the time. The volunteer arrived very quickly, gathered up the family, and took them to the shelter. It was an unnerving experience. I checked on the mother and daughter the following day, and was disappointed to hear that they had left the shelter early that morning. Though no one knew for sure, it was likely they went back to their home. The woman probably didn't think she really had any choice. However, they had acquired some valuable information about their rights and the support services that were available. The husband may also have learned something—she had the power to leave.

Battering husbands who speak both English and a native foreign language often do not allow their wives to learn English. Not allowing them to communicate in English is one of the ways to keep them dependent and reluctant to try to escape the situation. Also, a woman might be in the US on her husband's visa and could face deportation if she leaves him.

Sexual assault survivors have an even more difficult time convincing those who have not experienced the problem that they did not ask for it. The survivor is questioned about her clothing, makeup, if she was drinking, if she was with the attacker voluntarily, or if she had earlier sexual experiences. Rape survivors used to be asked if they had tried to fight the attacker. Like battered women, they often have to deal with distrust and suspicion from the police officer who is gathering evidence. Typically, the attacker is not a stranger but someone the survivor knows and was with voluntarily. They are hard cases to prosecute, but, just as they have done in response to domestic violence, women have organized, opened rape crisis hotline services, and provided support and accompaniment through the ordeal of reporting. Women were lacking these vital services in Houston until the women's center was created.

Women's groups all over the country have lobbied to have domestic violence and rape evidence laws changed and for the ability to participate in the training of officers. This is the political side of women's services. People and institutions have come to accept that government and criminal justice institutions have a crucial role to play in providing equality for women by helping to manage the violence against them.

Another major cause of misunderstanding these crimes is the assumption that whatever the circumstances, it "didn't really happen," that women make it up due to some motivation like a desire to even the score due to some imagined mistreatment. I often heard this allegation when I was out speaking, and it was not unusual to have it backed by some story someone had been told. I usually countered this belief with data. I talked about the number of calls that WIRES received each month or the number of women and children who had been in our shelter. I asked people to think about the circumstances that would drive women to leave their homes, usually with their children, and relocate in some unknown place among strangers. I asked them to think about the limited options they faced and the desperation that drove them. They typically could not turn to their families because that was the first place the abusers went to look for them, often threatening to hurt the family members as well.

Women at the shelter were responsible for caring for themselves and their children, including cooking and cleaning their rooms, assessing their longer-term situation, or perhaps seeking a protective order from the district attorney. They needed to consider divorce and check on permanent housing and employment. The decisions that had to be made were enormous. Unfortunately, they had to be made quickly, all while their past circumstances left them feeling bad about themselves, guilty about being abused, frightened, and hopeless about their future.

Most of the women who came to the shelter brought their children. There were usually as many or more children than women at the shelter. Typically, most of what these children had learned about adult men was that they could be violent. To try to change that image, we encouraged men to volunteer at the shelter with the children. The idea of children caught up in the violence was abhorrent to most people, so on some occasions when I was asked to give presentations to organizations for possible funding, I invited one of our best male volunteers to join me in the presentation. On one of these occasions, a male volunteer told the story of a three-year-old boy who had become seriously attached to him. One evening as the volunteer was explaining to the little boy that it was time for him to go home for the day, the boy got upset. The volunteer knelt down to try to calm him. The boy clenched his fist and hit the volunteer in the face with all his strength. "He was three years old," the volunteer told us. "He didn't injure me, but it didn't feel good either. He was a tough little guy. I used it as a teaching opportunity. I explained that I didn't want to be hit any more than he did. If he was going to hurt me, I would stop coming." The boy calmed down and begged him to come back. As the volunteer explained, hitting was all he knew. That was how he saw adult males get what they wanted. It was a compelling story. As I recall, we received the funding we were seeking that day.

Irvin eventually joined me at the shelter after he retired from Avis Rent-A-Car; he was a skilled carpenter and so he spent much of his time making repairs at the shelter and the women's center. One day he was using a wood-burning tool to make signs at the shelter. Before long he had attracted a fascinated audience of children. He asked them if they would like to each have a piece of wood with their name burned into it. They were thrilled with the prospect. He had them form a line and promised them they would each receive their names. The work took him the rest of the day. He didn't quite make it through the line, so he promised he would come back the next day to finish. They were waiting at the door when he arrived the next morning. He said, "As each one received their piece of wood with their name, they walked away staring intensely at it. It's hard to explain. Having their name on that wood seemed like the most valuable thing they had ever had. It was something that was all theirs because their name was on it. They sat down and just stared at it." The volunteers told him they had never had such quiet days in the shelter.

We housed children and women from many different groups at the shelter even though I heard over and over that "it doesn't happen" to us. I interpreted that version of the denial of violence against women as a kind of group pride: It doesn't happen to people like us. A short while after the first shelter opened, it was filled with Anglos and African Americans. I had a speaking engagement during that time to a Latina group. They inquired about the people occupying the shelter. I gave them some general information about who was there at the time, but I also explained that this kind of violence happened in all racial and ethnic groups and that anyone could be caught up in this kind of violence. Their response was that there would be no Latinas in the shelter because of their culture. They had strong families and managed their own problems within their communities. In about two weeks, the shelter was filled with Latinas. Another time I spoke to a Jewish organization. Once again, I was told that domestic violence didn't happen in the Jewish community. Their strong culture and religion precluded it. I knew better than that, because the lead volunteer at the shelter was a Jewish woman who had escaped a battering situation; her husband was well regarded in the Jewish community. On it went with theories about income, education, religion, race, and ethnicity. None of it held up. Domestic violence is an equal-opportunity crime because it is tied to the belief of some men that they have the right to dominate women. Like sexual abuse, the cause is domination and the abuse of power.

In our experience, many such abusers grew up in violent homes themselves. Even when they despised seeing their mother beaten, they still tended to internalize the message that men had the right to use violence in the family to get their way. Sometimes there wasn't even a disagreement. It just had to do with how they felt that day. I received a call once from the mother of a battered woman. The mother was beside herself. Her daughter was married with two children, one a toddler just learning to walk. The mother told me that her daughter had been resting, stretched out on her living room sofa with her hair hanging over the arm of the sofa. The toddler wandered over to the sofa, lost her balance, and grabbed her mother's hair as she started to fall. The mother reached back over her head to secure the toddler's hands and restrain her from pulling her hair. When she let go, the baby lost her balance again, landed on her rear, and began to cry. As she was rising from the sofa to calm the child, the father, who had been observing, flew out of his chair, grabbed his wife around the neck, and choked her until she started to lose consciousness. He threw her down on the floor, screaming that she was a miserable mother who deserved to be choked to death.

The mother of the abused woman was frantic. She told us this incident was typical of his behavior. She said that she and her husband could no longer take their daughter in anymore because the husband would come right over to their house, force his way in, threaten to kill them too, and drag her away. I told her about the shelter and warned her that her daughter needed to get out of the situation because it would only get worse. I don't know what happened after that. The person who is being abused has to make the call for help, since shelter personnel never know what situation they are facing and what disturbance they could cause by calling.

Organizations like the Women's Center were essentially shut out of the "old boys' network" and the funds that typically derive from those connections. However, in Houston, after the position of Women's Advocate was eliminated, those who supported the advocate idea turned their attention to the goal of getting women elected to office. Other women responded and began to seek elective office in greater numbers. Two women were elected to the city council, and a woman, Kathy Whitmire, was elected city controller. For the first time, I felt the benefits of having a woman near the political top. Kathy Whitmire informed me that funds had been donated to the city to be used for charitable purposes. Though they had been there for some time, no one had applied for them, probably because no one knew about them. I submitted an application, and it went through smoothly. For the first time, money came in on a regular basis, and that felt wonderful.

I anticipated that word about this source of funding would likely spread and we would have some competition for it. With input from my staff, I made the risky move of inviting the city council members to have lunch at the shelter. To my surprise, most accepted. I could tell they were all quite nervous when they arrived, as was I. The program director and volunteers did most of the talking, and after lunch we did a short presentation using data to make the case for the need for our services. We could see they were having a positive reaction, one we hoped would pay off over the long run. We were still received that funding when I moved on from the center.

We did have an amusing experience at that luncheon. Our presentation covered all of the services provided by the women's center, including that we served men as well as women. One of the younger council members challenged us. "You don't serve men in the rape crisis program." The presenter assured him that indeed we did. "Men can't be raped!" the council member exclaimed. The other council members broke into laughter. I and those of us from the women's center refrained from joining in the laughter. One of the older council members remarked, "Listen, son, let's just drop this subject for now. I'll explain it to you later." We were all rather shocked by this lack of knowledge. There were several red faces among the council members.

During another fundraising effort, I became better acquainted with the Greater Houston Community Foundation, which managed and provided funding to Houston charitable organizations. I had been speaking one day with former mayor Fred Hofheinz, who remained a friend, about the hardship of fundraising. He asked if I had applied to the Greater Houston Community Foundation. I said I had but was turned down. He told me that one of his best friends, who had been the driving force for setting up the foundation, was currently chairman of the board. Mayor Hofheinz then arranged for me to meet with Reuben Askanase. I told him about the women's center, and he encouraged me to submit another grant proposal. It was rapidly approved. Askanase became a loyal supporter of the women's center. It really helps to have friends in high places, or friends who have friends.

Those funds and other grants and donations helped the women's center to not only thrive but also grow. We were able to hire directors for all of the programs and purchase a larger shelter for the survivors of domestic violence. The structure of the organization changed as well. Initially, when the Houston Area Women's Center was established as an organization providing multiple services for women and their children, we brought together several existing organizations that were struggling to start providing services for victims of sexual assault, domestic violence, and other circumstances. The directors of these programs routinely looked to me as their supervisor, but the program volunteers still felt some agitation over having given up their identities and independent management to become part of a larger organization. That problem dissipated when we were finally able to hire a program supervisor to be head of program planning and the supervisor of the individual program directors. It was a big relief for me, and the organization became more stable.

After we met our three-year threshold of existence, we became eligible to apply for United Way funding. Following the submission of the paperwork, we met in person with some of their board members. They preferred meeting at the shelter, as it was that service in which they were most interested. We gathered at the appointed time, and the United Way representatives began asking questions. The nature of the questions seemed to imply that a domestic violence shelter wasn't as essential as we were making it out to be. Other kinds of shelters might be able to serve the same needs. The United Way was, understandably, wary of using their funds for duplicate services. But a domestic violence shelter isn't just a place for people to eat and sleep. It requires a broad range of services to help women and their children reshape their lives, and, unlike at other shelters, the most important service is security.

We were sitting in the living room of the shelter, where the chairs formed a circle at one end. Those of us from the women's center were facing the end of the room that led toward the kitchen and bedrooms. The residents had been told that visitors were coming from the United Way; one or two at a time they eased into the living area until they made a sizeable group. Sometimes the women who came to the shelter didn't show much evidence of having been battered. The bruising or injuries are often hidden by clothing or are just not visible for one reason or another. That was not the case at this time. One woman was on crutches, a couple of women had black eyes, and some wore bandages. They truly looked like they had come home from the war. The United Way representatives, whose chairs faced away from the residents, sensed that others were in the room and began turning around. Whatever questions they'd had about the need for a shelter for survivors of domestic violence were obviously answered. One of the biggest benefits of United Way funding was their willingness to provide funding for administrative needs. Most funding sources prefer to give money to programs rather than to administrative personnel: bookkeepers, clerks, and other essential workers who keep the programs running.

The biggest problem I struggled with aside from funding was locating adequate space for the women's center headquarters. By the mid-1980s, we were still in one large room at the UT School of Public Health that had originally been a study room for students. I'm sure they could have used it for either that or other purposes, but no one pressured us to leave. Housed in this room were the executive director, a bookkeeper, a secretary-assistant, WIRES (usually two or three people at a time), the director of the rape crisis program, and often a volunteer, the program supervisor, and two women who worked in community education (media, speaking engagements, and special events). The room was packed. We often spilled into the hallway when we held meetings. It was a lively place.

Occasionally I received calls from people offering us free or inexpensive property, usually with the shelter in mind. At first, I would take a look at the property every time I received an offer, but what I typically found was some trashed-out place that someone was trying to unload for a tax break. I learned to ask a few pointed questions and, depending on the answers, I would not waste my time going to look.

One day I received a call from a woman asking if I had gone to look at the property yet. She said she had called a couple of times about a property she thought would be perfect for the headquarters. I was a little embarrassed at having no memory of her previous calls. She said if I had the time, she would meet me over there right then. I agreed, somewhat skeptically. When I arrived, I was amazed to find a large old beautiful two-story brick building with a smaller two-story building behind it, which I assumed at one time had been quarters for the help.

The building was in need of repairs and maintenance. It hadn't been used for some time. Most recently it had been the headquarters for the type of women's club that modern life had passed by. No one held meetings in the building anymore. The woman who called had been charged with finding another use for it.

The more delicate fittings, such as a shapely banister and chandeliers in the living room area, had been removed. The walls were seriously damaged in places. The plan was to loan us the building at no charge, though the repairs and utilities would be our responsibility. I am not sure why they didn't sell the building, but I was certainly grateful that they hadn't.

I brought the idea of moving the headquarters of the women's center to the board of directors, and, to my surprise, I ran into quite a bit of resistance. They were concerned we might not be able to afford it and that by the time we faced that predicament, we would have lost our present space and be homeless, so to speak. I shared

A proud moment in front of the Houston Area Women's Center's new home.

Plaque honoring the founders at the entrance of the current headquarters of the Houston Area Women's Center.

their concern, but my thinking was that we were growing and we needed to find a location that would allow us to continue to grow. This move was relatively small in terms of adding to our expenses, but very large in terms of the possible benefits for our future. The property was in the Montrose area of Houston on a lovely little street called Chelsea Place. We would be able to put a sign in the front yard, which would provide us positive publicity. There was an intangible appeal as well—the place just looked like the home of the Houston Area Women's Center. It gave us dignity. It was sizeable enough to hold our board meetings and other types of functions. I won the battle on the side of growth, and we moved.

It was a tough move. We scrambled for volunteers, furniture, and various types of equipment. Bit by bit we repaired and dressed up the place. Irvin did a lot of the carpentry work. We had help from volunteers, but we also had to pay for some of the difficult repairs. When we finally got the banister and chandeliers back in place, I felt like the Houston Area Women's Center had found its home.

8 Electoral Politics

I am proud of the work I did at the Houston Area Women's Center. Sharing that work with the staff and volunteers as president of the board and executive director for nine years was, most of the time, joyful. The staff and volunteers were kind and dedicated people, and I had no doubt that I was involved in a very worthy cause. It was a difficult decision for me to consider taking a new direction in my life, but I was convinced by my experience with the Houston City Council that when women did not have fair representation a misogynistic attitude could easily prevail. That knowledge left me with a strong desire to run for a seat on the city council, where I would have more power to change my community into one that was fairer, more equal, and more dignified for those of us who were poorly represented. I believed it could be done, and I believed I could help do it.

In 1983, I decided to make my move. One of the city council members retired, leaving an open seat. In any governmental election, an open seat where there is no incumbent running for reelection offers the best opportunity to win, since an incumbent usually has a strong advantage. It looked like a good opportunity for me to enter the race. Of course, other people had the same idea. The fact that my name was well known was a positive factor; the fact that there were a considerable number of people who had negative thoughts about me was a problem.

When I was the Women's Advocate, Houston had a governing structure made up of a mayor, city controller, and five city council members who represented individual districts but were elected at-large. That is, everyone in Houston could vote for them, but they were responsible for representing only one district each. Three other council members were also elected at-large but represented the entire city. All elected officials held two-year terms.

By the time I ran for an at-large position on the city council in 1983, the membership had changed considerably and for the better. In the mid-1970s, a minority group had filed a voting rights lawsuit, resulting in the structure of the city council being changed. Instead of all council members being elected at-large, nine members were elected by voters in specific, or single-member, districts, and they directly represented those districts. Five members were elected at-large to represent the interests of the entire city. The total number of representatives was increased from eight to fourteen. That change in structure had the small but positive effect of more women and minorities being elected. Minority members increased from one to four (all men) because it was now possible to be elected from districts where minorities were the majority population. For the increase in women (from none to two, both Anglo), the expla- nation was a little more complex. The lawsuit seemed to have opened up the system, and I like to think that the ordeal of the Office of the Women's Advocate had served as a pointed reminder that women did not have any voice in the Houston City Council. Not one woman had been elected to office in city government until Kathy Whitmire was elected to a two-year term as city controller in 1978. It took until 1980 for women to be elected to the city council; that year Christin Hartung and Eleanor Tinsley took their seats on the council.

The first thing you have to ask yourself when thinking about running for office is, do I really want to do it? Even running for a local seat like city council is extremely demanding. That was not something I had to give a lot of thought to. The whole point of running is, of course, to win, and I had a lot of confidence. But before I made the commitment, I sought feedback from people who had experience and knowledge of running for and holding office. I knew I was going to have at least one strong opponent—he was a council member who currently held a seat in a single-member district but was going to run for the open at-large position.

The first person I spoke to about my ambition was former mayor Fred Hofheinz, as he knew the politics of the city extraor- dinarily well. He thought I had a reasonable chance of winning.

He encouraged me to enter the race and publicly endorsed my candidacy.

I also spoke to the council member leaving the position, Johnny Goyen, who had been appointed to fill the term of a council member who had died while in office. In spite of my difficult history with the council, he was very supportive and encouraging. He also endorsed me. I then met with a friend of mine who was a federal district judge. He was an older man, and for the several years I had known him, he had been my sounding board on many decisions. We didn't always agree, but he had many years of experience in the political world and I respected his judgment. His response to my proposed candidacy was, "Politics will break your heart." I knew that was probably true, but I didn't think it could be much worse than what I had already been through. I was wrong about that.

I confided in many people, including my husband. Candidacy takes a serious toll on the family. Anyone who runs for office needs the full support of members of the family. Irvin was excited about the prospect and willing to put up with the hardships. Neither of us knew exactly what we were getting into. No one advised me not to do it. Some were genuinely enthusiastic, others were wary. They all seemed to believe that I had a fairly good chance of winning, but several also warned me to keep my day job. I intended to do that. My plan was not to leave the women's center until I was elected to office. Most of the campaigning was in the evening and on weekends. I knew that in case I lost, which would cause real pain, I didn't want to also end up unemployed.

Going into the race, I was known as an advocate for women. I knew I would have to broaden that image by promoting policies that appealed to men and to different communities around the city. To be seen as a more responsive city council member, I talked about a better Houston, specifically promoting issues like better streets, improved traffic, control over taxes, safety and security, and a cleaner and more appealing environment. Houston has several bayous, or small rivers, running through it—I promoted the idea of cleaning them up and converting them to places of recreational enjoyment, for canoeing and kayaking. All this was not easy for me. I really wanted to be an elected city council member who was a women's advocate.

Seeking votes from members of a Hispanic women's group.

Campaign material promoting Van Hightower for city council.

Although I had a fairly close association with many elected officials, I had not been deeply involved in any political campaign. I was shocked at how much I didn't know and how uncomfortable I found much of it to be. For instance, after I made my announcement that I was running, I expected that people would naturally seek me out when I attended a function to inquire about what I was planning to do once in office. It was the other way around. I quickly discovered that I should be approaching them. My social skills were clearly limited when it came to campaigning.

There is a campaign tactic called "working the room," meaning that when attending an event you should move around the room, introduce yourself as a candidate, and talk to as many people as possible about something related (or not related) to the campaign. In comparable situations before I began campaigning, I would, after entering a room, seek out someone familiar and visit with them until someone else came along. But that approach meant I didn't talk to many people. After my first evening out, I was harshly criticized by a friend. "You didn't work the room. You just wasted the evening," he scolded. My excuse was that I didn't know many of the people who were there. "You don't have to know them, you have to get to know them. Getting people to know who you are is the point."

I was sort of shocked. People were investing in me, one way or another, and they wanted to see a good performance. I watched other candidates, marveling at how they moved through a room talking to almost everyone. Each conversation lasted a very short time. I forced myself to move in and introduce myself to strangers, but then I had problems breaking away. I still wasn't working the room. I called on my campaign manager for assistance. She and a close group of volunteers decided that I should always go to functions with one or two other people whose task would be to make sure I worked the room properly. It was called "staffing the candidate." I was always surprised at how much easier it was to work a room with at least one other person guiding me.

Being "staffed" accomplished a couple of things. My staffer was trained to get me in and out of conversations. To me it just seemed rather rude to intervene in a group's conversation to introduce myself and make a pitch for my candidacy. I was much more comfortable when someone else did the introductions and then ended the conversation by stating that someone else was waiting to meet me.

The other benefit of "staffing the candidate" was emphasizing that I had enthusiastic supporters around me. I have always been a physically small person, and when I got into the midst of a crowd I tended to disappear. But when I was with one or two other people who seemed positive about being near me, it gave me presence. Larger people have a great advantage in working a crowd. I couldn't change my size, but with a better strategy, I finally mastered the business of working the crowd. Another important result of being "staffed" is that it can help you appear to be truly enjoying yourself, even when you would much rather be home watching some mindless program on TV. People pick up on whether you would rather not be doing what you are doing, so it was important to remember that I was on stage.

One particular experience of working the room has stayed with me. I worked with a well-trained group of staffers who understood their roles and their obligation to the candidate. One afternoon I attended a function with a staffer who was a former student of mine. The event started out fine, but then, when I sensed it was time to move on, I looked around for him but he was nowhere to be seen. I felt the same old anxiety and began to wander around, forcing my way into groups until he finally showed up. I took him off to one side and reminded him what his job was. "Oh," he said, "I met the most interesting person. He knows everything about campaigning and politics. I think we should try to get him involved in the campaign."

"What is his name?" I asked. When he told me my jaw dropped. "He is one of my opponents!" I whispered angrily. He apologized profusely, but I had him removed from candidate staffing.

Most people have things in their past that they prefer not to deal with in public. A good campaign manager will advise you to get it out at the beginning of a campaign, so if and when your opponent brings it up, it will be treated as old news, particularly by the media. Such issues can be embarrassing at best and destructive to your campaign at worst. Examples of dangerous issues are things like drunken driving, illegal marijuana use, ugly divorces, issues related to children, financial matters such as bankruptcies, and false claims of accomplishments like degrees or awards. If most of them are revealed early, and you admit to mistakes you made earlier in your life, the coverage by the media is usually quite brief and sometimes sympathetic. When I was a candidate, a question not typically asked then in the 1980s, but most likely would be now in the 2010s, was about my religious beliefs. It was not brought up when I was running, so I didn't bring it up. In today's campaigns, people can always expect the question. I was once asked if I were a lesbian. I gave some noncommittal remark in reply like, "Not that I'm aware of." I am not a lesbian, but I didn't want to be caught in a denial that would imply that being a lesbian was a bad thing.

At that time, before the internet, there was only one reliable way for a candidate to make contact with the roughly 1.5 million citizens in an at-large district in Houston, and that was through broadcast and print media. One of the purposes of media time is to introduce yourself—your name, background, family, accomplishments. The fact that I was already well known through my activism helped me tremendously. However, my major opponent was also well known, having previously served on the city council. If one isn't fortunate enough to begin a campaign with strong name identification, it has to be promoted and purchased through very expensive media buys, though in smaller districts or towns, block-walking can be a quite sufficient way to meet constituents.

The media can be utilized effectively in a couple of ways. One way is free, and the other way isn't. Coverage is free when you are doing something the media considers to be of interest, so they have an incentive to cover you. When I was the Women's Advocate and head of the Houston Area Women's Center, I participated in lots of newsworthy activities without being particularly conscious of it, so, as a result, I gained significant name identification, even though it was not all positive. The media tends to be cynical when it comes to political candidates, viewing them as promoting their own personal ambitions. Politicians tend to receive media attention when they first announce their candidacy, sometimes when they gain note-worthy endorsements, when they have something negative to say about their opponents, or when they release a proposal for a major policy shift. Of course, free coverage is nearly guaranteed when an opponent has said something negative about you.

The only certain way to have the amount of positive media coverage you need is to buy it and place it on the air. Paid media costs a lot of money. In a sprawling city like Houston with multiple media outlets, time on each one had to be purchased separately because each reached different audiences. When I started out, I didn't realize how expensive it was going to be or how much time I was going to have to spend fundraising to meet those expenses. When I was fundraising on behalf of the women's center, I didn't find it particularly pleasant, but I had a strong sense of justification because I believed in the cause of the women's center. I found it much more difficult to raise funds for myself.

Candidates often hire fundraising specialists, but their main task is to compile lists of people who might be receptive to your requests. Almost every day I spent at least a couple hours on the phone asking for campaign donations. Much as I dreaded it, I did not complain. Being a candidate was my choice, and I didn't think it was right to burden my campaign manager or fundraising specialist with having to lean on me to do the job. Besides, I didn't want to show my anxiety and fear. On the days I concentrated on fundraising, I had to give myself a harsh talk about how I was capable of doing this, how it was in my interest to do it, and how being turned down was not going to kill me. Most of the people I talked to (if I could get them on the phone) were familiar with the game and wanted to have friends in city hall. Their challenge was predicting the winner, or, as they say, "picking the right horse."

Most candidates, male or female, find it unpleasant to fundraise, but in general, I believed the fundraising process was easier for men than for women. Most big contributors to campaigns were men. Women didn't give as often and they didn't give as much. Men, more so than women, appreciated the benefits of making sizeable campaign contributions, and men were more likely to feel free to make sizeable contributions without consulting their wives, whereas women usually conferred with their husbands. Aside from begging over the phone for campaign contributions, other sources of funding included direct mail to contributors (which

Announcement of a fundraising function with Ann Richards as the guest speaker. Courtesy of the Daily Politico.

Candidate, host, captivate crowd with savvy, wit

BOOMTOWN, USA: The Westin Oaks ballroom was truly *the* place to be seen when State Treasurer Ann Richards, that naughty gal from Austin, joined her long-time *amiga* Nikki Van Hightower for what proved to be the high spot of this year's political party circuit. Nikki, who is the favorite for the citywide council seat held by the highly supportive Johnny Goyen, was able to raise quite a bit of the cool green to add to her campaign war chest.

Radiant and fresh despite the rigors of campaign life, Nikki sparkled as excited throngs of the most politically astute mingled with the cream of Bayou City's corporate and social set. Admired by all present, the soon-to-be Councilmember held the crowd's attention with her ever- present charm and political savvy.

Sharing the spotlight with The Candidate was the effervescent Ann R., who herself became the state's political darling by a landslide during this hectic time last year. Flying in from Austin to host the event, the stunning state official proceeded to captivate the crowd with her special brand of humor and (gasp!) barbed wit.

Ms. Richard's support lends a special aura to the highly impressive list of campaign supporters and volunteers that have drawn together to place Nikki Van Hightower's expertise where it belongs—in the corridors of City Hall.

Today's photo stars: State Treasurer Ann Richards (upper) and City Council candidate Nikki Van Hightower.

Editors

Jim Box
David Burchfield
Jerry Finger
Johnny Goyen
Howard Horne
Leonard Rauch
Kenneth Schnitzer

usually resulted in small contributions), campaign events such as luncheons or evening parties, and other social activities. People would pay to attend such events, but the big money came from various levels of sponsorships, which at that time were generated in the familiar way—fundraising by telephone.

In addition to the cost of paid media, the expenses of campaigning included salaries, rent for campaign headquarters, and money to create signs, bumper stickers, and various kinds of printed materials. By the end of my city council campaign, I had raised about $250,000. The overall campaign expenses included a runoff election with an opponent who, because he had held a single-member district seat previously, was able to raise money much like an incumbent. That is, he had been responsive to people's requests during his tenure, and this was payoff time.

The runoff election would take place about six weeks after the first election, meaning that everything would have to start up again: more fundraising, more media, more events, and more paid staff. Our at-large race was the only one that resulted in a runoff (because none of us had received over 50 percent of the vote), which meant that turnout would be low. Fortunately, we received a fair amount of media attention.

My opponent had been one of the two African American winners in the new single-member district seats that had resulted from the lawsuit over voting rights. The mandated changes from the lawsuit brought the total number of African American members on the council to three. If my opponent lost the race to me, the number of African Americans would shrink to two. As this would be considered a major loss for the black community their motivation was very high to vote in the runoff election for my opponent. Unfortunately, the same consideration did not apply to women.

Runoff elections are always tricky. The candidate who is most able to lure their earlier voters back to the polls has a huge advantage and usually wins.

Women were just beginning to enter the phase in their political history when they appreciated the benefits of having their sex represented in public office. They had not developed the same kind of unified political organization as had African Americans, which was probably one of the reasons I lost the election. There was a large turnout of African Americans in the runoff although the overall turnout was low, which was typical.

It is difficult to describe how painful that loss was. I tried not to show it, but I felt like screaming. I called my opponent the night of the election after the returns were in to congratulate him on his win. The conversation was short and sweet, all I could handle at the time. He was very gracious. The following morning during a TV interview I once again congratulated him and, on behalf of all the citizens of Houston, wished him success in his term. I certainly wasn't going to make myself vulnerable to being labeled a sore loser. The pain, however, didn't recede. My campaign manager left immediately after the election on a trip, and volunteers turned their attention to other things, leaving Irvin and me to clean up the headquarters, return borrowed furniture, and try to raise a little more money to pay off bills.

A large sum of money, in the form of loans to my campaign from businessmen who wanted to have friends on city council, was never paid back. I shared my agony over not being able to pay off those debts with Johnny Goyen, a friend and former city council member. He gave me some helpful reassurance: "Nikki, these are big boys. They've been around the block. They know the risks. Just quit worrying about it." It wasn't quite that easy, but essentially that is what I did.

I charged back into my work at the women's center to get my mind off the loss. Time and work at the women's center helped. I made a point of calling friends and having lunch with them and talking. I swore to myself and to others that I would never run for office again.

As they say, never say never.

In 1986, three years after I ran for city council, George Strong, the campaign manager of my former opponent, contacted me to encourage me to run for treasurer of Harris County, where Houston is located. He believed the incumbent had not established much name identification among the citizens of Harris County and could be easily beaten. This was another lesson for me: You don't stop campaigning once you have been elected.

In spite of what I had said three years earlier, I was interested. It was not so much that I wanted to be the county treasurer. I wanted a career in politics. The treasurer was not a policy-making office, but it was a foot in the door.

This would be a different kind of race for me because it was partisan. Town and city elections in Texas are nonpartisan, so you

Lapel pin for campaign for Harris County treasurer.

Block-walking with supporters during the race for Harris County treasurer.

run on the strength of your name and background, like I did for city council. In partisan races, you run on your name, of course, but you also run under a party label. First you run in a primary election against other members of your party. If you win, you become your party's candidate. In my case, I ran against other Democrats to become the Democratic candidate. The next step is to run in the general election against the winner of the race in the other party, in this case Republican.

I wasn't as familiar with county government as I was with city government. However, I was familiar with the Harris County commissioners and the county judge—all white males until El Franco Lee, an African American and former state representative, was elected in 1984. Most people are not familiar with county government, so once elected the county officials tended to stay for as long as they wanted. Each one of the four commissioners was somewhat similar to a mayor in the kind of power they held in the precincts they represented. The powers of the county judge, who was elected at large, were fairly weak compared to the county commissioners. Other elected officials in the county were sheriff, district attorney, county attorney, tax assessor/collector, county clerk (at that time, the only elected woman in Harris County), county treasurer, four justices of the peace, and four constables. Most of the county's governing work was done outside the boundaries of city government. The county treasurer shared money management responsibilities with the appointed county auditor. Money came in and was managed and distributed from the treasurer's office. About fifteen people worked in the treasurer's office, including the treasurer.

The treasurer's race was much easier and much less expensive than the race for city council. I had some opponents in the primary, but they were not well known, so not terribly threatening. I relied heavily on campaign functions that were arranged by other Democratic candidates in the "meet and greet" category. My previous experience from the city council race helped enormously. I knew how to work a room, although I still relied on being "staffed" when I attended most functions.

I easily won the primary and then the general election. In this race, I almost enjoyed running for office. What I didn't enjoy was holding the office. The four commissioners and county judge made sure my life was miserable. In the time between my winning the election and taking office, most of the important money management functions were removed from the treasurer's office and relocated to the auditor's office, which was not a welcoming experience.

Since all of the remaining responsibilities were new to me, I knew I needed some help to sort things out. For the role of my assistant I hired a certified public accountant who was brilliant and helped me figure out what was going on. It was clear that the commissioners and county judge did not want to have to deal with me when it came to the management of county money. Apparently, it had been a cozier arrangement under the former treasurer. Because the commissioners had hired the auditor, they had a great

Congratulating new treasurer

Chronicle 1-2-87

Carlos Antonio Rios / Chronicle

Houston Area Women's Center founder Nikki Van Hightower is hugged by attorney and former Mayor Fred Hofheinz after she was sworn in Thursday as Harris County treasurer at Commis- sioners Court courtroom. As the county treasurer, a post she won in the November elections, Van Hightower will oversee the deposit and disbursement of millions in county funds.

Congratulations from former mayor Fred Hofheinz at the swearing-in for Harris County treasurer.

deal more control over him than over me. The money still came into the office and went out of the office in the form of checks, but the management affairs, such as the banking and investments, were out of my hands.

I expressed outrage to the court members, but to no avail. They just ignored me. I spoke to the county attorney and the auditor. No one wanted to get snarled up in the issue. Finally, in the summer of 1987, I went to the banks that held the county's money. I told them if I were not given more control, I would stop signing checks. (Actually, the thousands of checks that went out were signed by a machine, but the machine used my signature only on my authority.) This got the banks' attention because they knew I had the legal power to follow up on my threat and what a mess could result.

Steve Friedman of the *Houston Chronicle* reported what happened:

> In a move that could wrestle power from the county auditor, Harris County Treasurer, Nikki R. Van Hightower wrote four local banks Monday saying state law requires instructions from her office before any action is taken with most county funds.
>
> County officials said the action could force the banks to freeze roughly $500 million now on deposit, which includes employee payroll funds, because of conflicting instructions. The banks had been told that County Auditor Joe Flack has authority to handle investments.

"Treasurer Refuses to Compromise on Duties," was the headline of John Mecklin's article in the *Houston Post*:

> Harris County Treasurer Nikki Van Hightower on Tuesday refused a compromise offer from County Judge Jon Lindsay in her fight to regain duties transferred to the county auditor.
>
> In turn, Lindsay threatened to send the dispute to court, claiming Van Hightower's action would shut down county financial operation.

"The boys" got together and offered me a reasonable compromise. All responsibilities would be returned except the full power to invest money that wasn't immediately transferred out as payments. That work was to be shared with the auditor's office. I could have pushed it further, but I was concerned about the chaos that would result if I actually held up payments from the county. At least I had an efficient and loyal staff.

The budget process in county government was much easier than in the city, where the entire city council publicly debated the budget for months. In the county, all department heads sent in their requests, which were compiled behind the scenes by the commissioners court and their assistants. The resulting budget was available for public review and comment for a week before it was voted on. There was very little conflict because the elected officials got pretty much what they wanted in a "go along to get along" arrangement. Since checks and balances were largely non-existent, things typically moved very smoothly.

A surprise fiftieth birthday party for the treasurer. The employees were the one bright spot of the treasurer's office.

The monster budget sat on a table outside the commissioners court for anyone interested in reviewing it. During my last year in office, I turned to the section on my department and to my surprise found that I had been given a $20,000 pay increase. Then I noticed that all elected officials had been given substantial increases. Mine was the smallest compared to the others. Nothing had been said publicly about this change. County officials were well paid compared to city officials. It was not as if they were going hungry. Ironically, there was constant talk of having to cut back on services due to lack of funds. I found it to be a sleazy move and decided not to accept the increase. I held a press conference to announce my decision just prior to the public discussion of the budget and then went to the commissioner's court meeting. The officials were not happy.

Some of the elected officials got in the line of people who were commenting on the budget and thanked the commissioners and county judge for their well-deserved salary increases. Aside from a few jabs by the media, that was the end of that. The *Houston Business Journal* made the following comment on their editorial page:

> Worst of all, the commissioners spat in the faces of Harris County's rank-and-file employees. By offering most county workers a 2 percent pay hike while granting themselves a 23.5 percent raise, commissioners have dealt a devastating blow to the morale of our county's employees.
>
> Actually, the commissioners should take lessons from county treasurer Nikki Van Hightower, who blasted the commissioners' pay raise as an obscenity. Van Hightower announced she personally would accept a raise of only 2 percent.

I spent a very isolated four years in county government. It was not what I had imagined. I attempted to bring some visibility to the treasurer's office since it was an elected position and I thought the public should be familiar with it. I started sending out newsletters informing people about the work of the office and how their money was handled. I still received many requests for public speaking, which I gladly accepted.

It wasn't a happy time. Just before I was elected county treasurer,

"Year One Annual Report," prepared by Nikki Van Hightower, Harris County treasurer.

Irvin and I divorced, though we continued to remain good friends. Then, just after I was elected, I learned that the bookkeeper at the women's center had not been making payroll tax payments to the IRS for over a year, which resulted in a major setback to the women's center. There was no money stolen; the accountant just decided on her own that not enough money was coming in and stopped making IRS payments, hoping that revenues would improve. This resulted in severe IRS penalties, job losses, and a

couple years spent straightening it out. I was personally embarrassed that something like this had happened under my watch,
particularly just as I was elected Harris County treasurer. It also
put a nasty stain on the women's center, an ugly situation I thought
I would never overcome, but I did. And I learned some important
lessons about trust. I had considered the bookkeeper not only a
trustworthy employee, but a good friend. I came out of the ordeal a
great deal more cautious than I went in. I had relied on the bookkeeper and an outside auditor to keep me informed about any
financial problems that needed my attention. I thought we had
adequate checks and balances. In retrospect, I also wondered why
the IRS did not notify us in a more timely manner that our payroll
taxes were not being submitted.

In 1990, the last year of my four-year term as Harris County
treasurer, the state treasurer, Ann Richards, announced that she
would not be running again but would be running for governor
instead. The gubernatorial incumbent, Bill Clements, had chosen
not to run again. Clements was a Republican, but almost all other
state office holders were Democrat, including Richards. Texas had
been a largely Democratic state since Reconstruction following the
Civil War, but it was changing. Ideological conservatives, who had
been Southern Democrats, were shifting their affiliations to the
Republican Party. Southern liberals were moving their loyalties
to the Democratic Party. Much of this change was related to the
issue of race under the term "states' rights." A segment of the
Democratic Party had become strong supporters of civil rights
starting in the Kennedy and Johnson administrations. As a result,
African Americans shifted their loyalties from the party of Lincoln
to the party of civil rights, the Democratic Party. Hispanics had a
low voter turnout but tended to split their votes between the two
parties, and Anglos were shifting from Democrats to Republicans.

With Ann Richards running for governor and leaving the
state treasurer seat open, I decided I would run for it. I was the
treasurer of the largest county in Texas, which I thought gave me
important credentials. I also wanted to get out of the Harris County
Treasurer's Office but remain in politics, and this seemed like the
perfect opportunity. Once again, I started calling people to get their
advice and opinions. The first person I called was Ann Richards.

I considered her a friend and a supporter. She and I had worked together in organizing the IWY state and national conferences, and both of us had served as Texas representatives to the national IWY conference in Houston.

I didn't receive the enthusiasm I hoped for. Her first response was, "Can you raise a million dollars?" I frankly did not know whether I could or not. She also warned me that it was very difficult running a statewide race. The warnings were a bit unnerving, but I took them as an act of friendship. Once again, my mind and heart were set on doing this, and I was determined. Since the county elections were at the same time, I would no longer be the county treasurer. My term would be over at the end of the year. Richards might have had some information about who else was going to enter the race that would make it very tough for me, but she didn't say. As it turned out, the candidate on the Republican side was Kay Bailey Hutchison, who had served in the state legislature until she ran for and lost a congressional seat. Before that she had been a television reporter in Houston, where she was still quite well known.

I made my announcement, and from the beginning it was rough. Like county government, the election was partisan, which meant candidates first had to win primaries to enter the general election as the party nominee. Since the treasurer's seat would be open, there were several people who decided to give it a try. As it turned out, my strongest opponent on the Democratic side was a man from West Texas who had held public office before at the local level. He was well known in his area.

Like Ann Richards said, a statewide race is difficult. It is costly and exhausting, especially in a state like Texas. Raising money in a primary was demanding because the contributors wanted to know for certain who the candidate was going to be in the general election. Although I had pretty decent statewide name recognition, most people outside of the Houston and Harris County area did not know much about me, so they weren't eager to hand over money. I spent the primary traveling around and introducing myself. I relied on local Houston contributors to accumulate start-up money.

The other candidates split up the race enough to keep any of us from gaining 50 percent of the vote. Although I was leading the other candidates, I still had to participate in a runoff, which, for

Fundraiser at the home of former governor Mark White, with supporter and guest speaker Colorado Congresswoman Pat Schroeder (far right).

all intents and purposes was another election. I had lost the city council race in a runoff, and the memories were unnerving. To my great relief, I won the primary runoff easily.

When the primary was finally over, the work started all over again, except now I needed a much larger staff and the fund-raising had to be much more expansive. In a partisan statewide race, the office of the state treasurer is toward the bottom of a long ballot. That didn't seem so bad because there were a lot of strong

Democrats above me. However, right above me on the Democratic side of the ballot was Jim Hightower, candidate for commissioner of agriculture, who was running against Rick Perry, the Republican candidate for the seat. It was a tight race between the two of them. I didn't know at the time that Jim, a friend of mine, did virtually no fundraising and spent very little on the race. Rick Perry, however, raised and spent a substantial amount of money.

Nevertheless, with such a strong ticket above me, I thought both of us would benefit. But Ann Richards was having problems as well in the general election. Her Republican opponent was Clayton Williams, a multi-millionaire and West Texas oilman, who spent twice as much money on the campaign. Richards was counting heavily on a loyal coalition of women and minority voters. Nevertheless, well into the campaign she was running behind.

Then Williams made some serious mistakes. On one occasion at an outdoor event for journalists at his ranch, someone made a comment about the rainy weather. Williams, who was subsequently quoted in the *New York Times*, compared the weather to rape, joking that "if it's inevitable, just relax and enjoy it." Women were offended by the remark, and the polls showed that he lost a large number of women voters. Then the *Washington Post* reported on his bragging about visiting houses of prostitution in Mexico, treating it as if women were meant to "service" men. Richards ended up carrying about two-thirds of the Hispanic vote even though Williams spoke fluent Spanish and had campaigned hard in South Texas. There was also an ugly moment following a debate when he refused to shake hands with Richards. It made him appear petty and ungentlemanly. At the conclusion of the campaign, Williams responded to a reporter's questions about his comments relating to women; for this he was quoted again in the *New York Times*, saying that one lesson he had learned from the campaign was "not to joke about the weather." If that was the lesson he learned, his loss was certainly understandable. Ann Richards won the race with 52 percent of the vote, and in 1991, she became the governor of Texas.

My campaign manager was counting on minority votes across the state, voters from Houston who had supported me for county treasurer, women voters who shared my position on women's rights, and Hispanic voters in South Texas. Opposition research had turned up Hutchison's legislative voting record on Hispanic issues, revealing that she had voted against some key policies related to bilingual voting rights and education. I made good use of that information when I campaigned in South Texas and did very well there. Where I didn't do very well was in the suburbs of Dallas and Houston.

All of the Democrats won in the statewide races except Jim Hightower and me. It was the last time Democrats would see that kind of victory. I lost by a little over 3 percent. It is hard to say how much Jim Hightower's race affected mine, but there was no doubt that it hadn't helped. A lot of people thought we were related or married. Texas was becoming a Republican one-party state, as was reflected in the next election in 1994 when most of the Democratic winners of 1990 lost. Also, I had only been able to raise $250,000, about the same as I raised for the Houston City Council race, and my opponent had raised close to $1 million.

It was another hard loss, except that this time I had no job waiting for me and my prospects looked pretty grim. But I was glad to see Ann Richards win and know the impact that women and minorities had had on the race. It was another step toward women being taken more seriously as voters and as candidates.

9 Teaching

Once again, I felt the pain of losing a political campaign, only this time a job wasn't waiting to help me pick up the pieces. Once again, I owed debts that couldn't be paid. The words of my friend the federal judge, who warned me that politics would break my heart, came back to haunt me. He was right. On the other hand, if you take risks in your life, you are going to get your heart broken now and then. I had lost before and life had gone on then, just as I knew it would again. For about a year I longed to get back into politics until I finally began to accept that the stars were not aligned for me and that I had to focus my attention on earning a living.

I spent the year of 1990 looking for employment. I had a friend on the Board of Regents at Texas A&M University whom I reluctantly called upon for assistance. She was very accommodating, introducing me to university administrators, yet even with her recommendation I was skeptical anything would come of it.

Texas A&M was well known as a politically conservative institution. Due to my reputation as an activist for liberal and feminist causes, I didn't expect to have the doors thrown open for me. At its founding, the Agricultural and Mechanical College of Texas, as it was called, was established to be all-male and all-white. The entire student body participated in military training in the Corps of Cadets. Change didn't come until the mid-1960s, and it didn't come easily. There was a considerable amount of resistance, particularly to admitting women. To my good fortune, the university was working hard to improve its image and encourage openness, equality, and diversity. Instead of being a liability, my background suited this mission.

I accepted the first position I was offered, assistant director of university relations, the university's public relations department.

While in that position, I was honored to receive several awards for publications I designed or helped design, but it was not the kind of work that was particularly meaningful to me.

When I arrived at the university, I made an appointment with the head of the political science department, Charles Johnson, about the possibility of teaching a course in addition to my job in University Relations. He was interested in someone with my background, so he offered me two courses a year, one each semester: Texas State and Local Government and Women and Politics. I was delighted. Compared to when I first started teaching at the University of Houston in 1975, I found the experience this time around to be remarkably positive. At UH, I had mainly relied on textbook knowledge, but in 1992, I benefitted from years of experience in the political world. Also, when I had taught before, there were no courses on women and politics nor did women's studies programs exist. The time away from academia worked to my benefit. In a way, time had finally caught up with my academic and political knowledge and interests.

After a couple of years working in University Relations and teaching courses in political science, I decided to make a rather dramatic change. I kept my teaching load at Texas A&M but left University Relations, instead accepting a position at Lee Community College teaching introductory courses in political science at the men's prison units in and around Huntsville, Texas. I taught five courses a semester at multiple units. Each course met once a week for three hours. I commuted to Huntsville, about fifty miles each way to teach for long hours. The job was physically demanding, but it was also interesting and educational. By that time I had considerable confidence in my teaching skills so I was not easily intimidated. I found it to be rewarding work.

Most inmates knew they had messed up their lives and were determined to make changes. The majority of students were from poor and minority backgrounds. Many had dropped out of the public school system, meaning that before they could begin their college work they had to take the courses they needed in order to receive their GEDs. The inmates took the classes voluntarily. On the whole, they were eager to learn. There were always a couple of characters who liked to expose themselves in class; I simply had them removed. Guards were posted very near the classrooms, so I felt quite well protected. Mostly I couldn't help but feel sorry for these men whom I knew had suffered a lot of hardships in their lives, and I admired them for their determination to educate themselves in hopes of finding something better. The Lee College director told me that recidivism was almost nonexistent among those who had enrolled in college classes while they were in prison.

In addition to teaching in the prison system and in the political science department, I was asked by the Texas A&M School of Medicine to teach a course on family violence. The class would only meet one morning a week for an hour, so I was quite sure I could handle it. The feedback from the medical students was mixed. I had the impression that a few of them thought learning about family violence was beneath them. I suppose I shouldn't have been surprised. One reason the medical school was offering the course in the first place was because they realized that battered women were rarely asked by doctors what had caused the problems presented to them, let alone if there was violence in their home. That lack of interest caused women to believe that violence against them was not a serious enough matter, or at least would not be taken seriously enough, for them to expect or rely on the concern of the medical establishment.

The academic areas of medicine and public health at Texas A&M eventually grew into the Texas A&M Health Science Center, which included the schools (now colleges) of medicine, dentistry, nursing, pharmacy, and rural public health (now public health). In 1996, after a year of teaching family violence in the School of Medicine, I accepted an offer to relocate to the School of Rural Public Health, teach courses on family violence, and develop services for victims of family violence in rural communities. I left the prison system to take the position of visiting assistant professor. I continued teaching in the department of political science.

Based on my experience in Houston, one of the major problems we had to overcome in order to provide effective services for battered women was that of biased attitudes in the criminal justice system. In Houston, we had made tremendous inroads. The women's center regularly participated in officer training programs, developing their trust and understanding in providing security for the shelter. We worked with the state legislature to strengthen the laws regarding family violence and were successful in having it reclassified as a serious criminal offense.

I began working on an initiative called the Program for the Reduction of Rural Family Violence. The goal was to organize volunteer family violence services in the rural counties surrounding Brazos County, where the university is located. My thinking was to use the startup of the Houston Area Women's Center as a model. I partnered with a TAMU graduate student in the field of sociology who was working on her dissertation on rural family violence.

Our first step was to assess the attitudes and responses of the criminal justice systems to domestic violence calls. Law enforcement officers were remarkably open in sharing their thoughts with us. Their attitudes reminded me of the early 1970s in Houston and Harris County. They were based less on updated laws and more on old stereotypes about battered women. The officers would often say things such as, "They ask for it by mouthing off to their husbands," or "They could leave if they wanted to." The old familiar excuses for neglecting to intervene went on and on: "These cases are particularly dangerous for criminal justice officials, because when we try to intervene the woman takes the side of the husband and attacks the officer," or "If she did leave, she would be right back and it would start all over again." Often the response to family violence calls was to not show up at all or to show up and get the couple calmed down only to leave them alone to make up. Sometimes the batterer was a peace officer assaulting his wife, with other officers covering for him.

After some negotiation, we were able to begin participating in the officer training programs. It was important that the volunteer program and law enforcement officials worked cooperatively. Typically, it was the law enforcement officials who were first called to a domestic violence scene, and, if things worked properly, an arrest would be made and then they would contact the domestic violence volunteer organization to make contact with the survivor. The volunteers would explain her rights, provide emotional support, and let her know about shelters in the area that she and her children might want to go to for safety.

To establish the domestic violence programs and prepare new

volunteers, we wrote a domestic violence training manual that would serve as the base of knowledge to be used for training everyone. We began to identify the women who were leaders in their communities. With the guidance of those leaders, we solicited other people who might like to be volunteers with the program. At the first training meeting, each volunteer was given a copy of the training manual. We had several evenings of training for the volunteers and also a monthly meeting at the School of Rural Public Health for the program leaders from all the counties where we were working.

We started out with a goal of organizing six or seven county programs. However, only three were able to sustain themselves. It became evident to me that we weren't going to be able to replicate the Houston model, at least in every case. In Houston the volunteers self-selected themselves to build the program, with the vast majority of them having firsthand experience in family violence. Working with local leaders in the rural counties, we recruited volunteers for the program, not all of whom were as firmly committed as this kind of work called for. The three programs that survived and grew did so because the skilled leaders were dedicated to the cause, having themselves experienced family violence, primarily in their own lives. One of the outstanding leaders worked for her county government as the victim assistance coordinator.

I believed that at least part of the reason for the differences I saw in motivation and commitment related to how volunteers interpreted the cause of family violence. In Houston, we had all shared an ideological commitment based on feminism. The HAWC was a feminist organization, part of the women's rights movement. That meant that service to survivors involved more than just ending the violence. It involved promoting a fundamental change in the relationship between women and men.

Under the feminist perspective, the battering phenomenon was based on a misguided belief that it was natural and legitimate for men to dominate or have power over women. To bring the violence to an end, attitudes had to change. Women had to have the ability to stand up for themselves, protect themselves, and be willing to exercise their rights. It involved demanding equality. The benefit of the battered women's shelter was to provide safety for the survivor and her family and to give her an opportunity to redirect her life. It was also to send a message to the batterer that he could no longer control her through violence and intimidation. She had rights that she could exercise. It was also important that the shelter worked closely with the criminal justice system, which was another way of teaching the batterer that his behavior was criminal and as such would not be tolerated by the community. This wasn't just a matter of a stormy relationship between a man and a woman.

In the rural family violence programs, a strong religious outlook existed among many of the volunteers. They did not necessarily reject the concept of male dominance and power. Their concern was what was done with that dominance and power. In other words, the patriarchal (male dominant/female subservient) system was tolerated as a moral system as long as men used their power to provide safety, economic support, and moral leadership for the family.

There was never any discord generated by these two different outlooks, but I personally felt uncomfortable with the religious approach because it left women vulnerable to the motives of the batterer and his interpretation of what was moral and not moral. From the feminist perspective, we strongly believed that violence against women was only one aspect of the abuse of power by men over women that needed to be eliminated.

I continued teaching part-time in the department of political science until 2001, when Charles Johnson, still the head of the department, offered me a full-time position as a senior lecturer. I accepted the position with the agreement that I could continue working with the rural family violence program and with the graduate student who was assisting me. I raised all the money myself for that program through foundation grants. In other words, the rural family violence program was fully funded by outside money.

When I started the rural family violence program, the idea was that I would stay involved until the individual county programs were stable and could run without me. Since some of them were struggling, I wasn't exactly sure when that would be, but as it turned out it wasn't my decision to make. Johnson was promoted to dean of the College of Liberal Arts, and a new department head was appointed. I needed her approval for the grants I was pursuing, but she was not happy with the program I wanted to fund. She claimed that it was not "political," as in "political science." We argued this point. My position was that family violence was certainly a political matter. Although it could also be studied under other disciplines as well, it related directly to the power structure in society, and that was political. In addition, the issue of domestic violence involved the law, the criminal justice system, and community organizing.

I lost the battle. Since I was unable to raise funds for the program as a result, I decided it was time for me to bow out. Three of the county programs were solid and had good leadership, even if the survival of the others was questionable. I could only hope that the volunteers would stick with it.

I taught two courses per semester in political science until I retired in 2011: Politics of State and Local Government and Women and Politics. In 2004 and 2005, I served as the interim director of the Women's and Gender Studies Program. My affiliation with that program, which offered both undergraduate and graduate degrees, was a satisfying ending to my career.

I never anticipated that my career would develop as it did. For that matter, in my younger years I had never anticipated that I would even have a career. At times I felt very much like an outsider. I now accept my outsider fate, as did those who worked with me. We were forcing change that was resisted by the insiders. My ambition took me to places where women were not welcomed. Even when I pushed, I was still not allowed in. I remained a foreigner. In many places in our society, even though we have made great progress, it will take a long time for women to be welcomed as equal partners.

Ten years ago, I attended the thirtieth anniversary banquet for the Houston Area Women's Center. During the program, the CEO of one of Houston's major banks stood up to thank the Women's Center for its valuable contribution to the community. He stated, "I can't imagine Houston without the Houston Area Women's Center." I nearly fell out of my chair. We certainly had made some progress.

In retirement, I've had time to reflect on the way I have conducted my life and career. I readily admit I have made mistakes, but I am confident I have been on the right side of history in my struggles for equal rights for women. My greatest pride is the Houston Area Women's Center. It now fills two large buildings, one for the shelter and one for the headquarters and all other services. It has two

24-hour hotlines, one for domestic violence and one for sexual assault. In 2016, the two hotlines received 42,553 calls. Also during 2016, more than 2,100 people found residence at the shelter—40 percent of them were children.

The man I worked with in the Affirmative Action Division in Houston city government who provided me with personnel data when no one else would, Raul Castillo, has become my life partner. We have a home in College Station, and we stay involved in the political issues we both continue to care about.

On January 20, 2018, the day after Donald Trump was inaugurated president of the United States, women marched throughout the country. A crowd estimated at 400,000 to 500,000 composed mostly of women marched at the US capitol. In Houston, former Mayor Annise Parker and activist Robin Paoli wrote a moving article in the *Houston Chronicle* entitled "Houston Women Are Marching Again: Here's Why." The article begins:

> Once, an all-male Houston City Council cut the salary of the lone woman advising them on equality and justice to $1 a year. Why? Because in 1977 Dr. Nikki Van Hightower spoke

Happy moment with my life partner, Raul Castillo.

in favor of the Equal Rights Amendment and "never consults with us about anything," the men said.

Hightower didn't quit. She spoke her mind. She didn't ask permission. She was punished, yet she persisted.

As we prepare for the second Women's March in Houston, this Saturday, Jan. 20, 2018, what's different from last year and from 40 years ago? Why are we marching in 2018? We march because women are still "less than" in America. Men make more money, hold more elected offices, lead more companies, make more laws, are quoted more frequently and have more screen time in movies. Are men that much worthier than women? No. Women are just as worthy as men, but women are not treated with equity, so we persist and march for equal rights under the law.

As I celebrate my eightieth birthday in the summer of 2019, I cannot help but reflect on those eighty years and ask myself, "What was that all about?" There are times when I allow myself to dwell on the denial of opportunities or the abuses I experienced as a female. I don't stay there long before my thoughts jump back to the opportunities that those experiences afforded me: to take risks, to greatly expand my skills, to become acquainted with valuable role models, and, amazingly, to become a role model for others. I have had the unique luxury of being part of a movement to bring about the kind of change that opened new doors for people's lives.

I sometimes slip into the darker places of thinking that I could have handled things better, that I could have accomplished more, and that I allowed my anger instead of my intellect to guide me. Fortunately, I don't always have to be my own judge. Others who are more objective can play that role.

Stored in the University of Houston library archives is a historical note about my career and activism in Houston: "Throughout her career, Van Hightower received numerous honors and awards and established an impressive vita of community involvement, publications, speaking engagements, and teaching appointments. Her refusal to be intimidated by the 'old boy' political network, which she viewed as a fundamental obstacle to equality and justice, enabled her to implement significant changes for the citizens of Houston."

I was surprised and gratified to find this assessment of my contributions, and I hope that I and all the others who worked so hard to gain a measure of equality have set an example of feminism that inspires and motivates women everywhere.

Sources

Angelou, Maya. "To Form a More Perfect Union." In United States National Commission on the Observance of International Women's Year. *The Spirit of Houston: The First National Women's Conference: An Official Report to the President, the Congress and the People of the United States*. Washington, DC: National Commission on the Observance of International Women's Year, Superintendent of Documents, US Government Printing Office, 1978, 195.

"Anne Forer Pyne, a Feminist Who Opened Eyes, Dies at 72," *New York Times* Obituaries, March 30, 2018. Accessed September 29, 2019. https://www.nytimes.com/2018/03/30/obituaries/anne-forer-pyne-a-feminist-who-opened-eyes-dies-at-72.html.

Austin American-Statesman, March 12, 1977.

Beauvoir, Simone de. *The Second Sex.* Translated and edited by H. M. Parshley. Jonathan Cape: London, 1953.

Berriozábal, Maria Antonietta. *Maria, Daughter of Immigrants.* San Antonio: Wings Press, 2012, 212, 214.

Catt, Carrie Chapman. Speech at 1920 convention of the National Woman Suffrage Association, quoted in Eleanor Flexner and Ellen Fitzpatrick. *Century of Struggle: The Woman's Rights Movement in the United States* 3rd rev. ed., enlarged. Cambridge, MA: Belknap Press, 1996, 320.

Cottrell, Debbie Maulden. "National Women's Conference, 1977." Texas State Historical Association, Handbook of Texas. Accessed September 28, 2019. https://tshaonline.org/handbook/online/articles/pwngq.

Declaration of Sentiments and the report of the Women's Rights Convention at Seneca Falls. Rare Book and Special Collection Division, Library of Congress, Washington, DC.

Dowd, Matthew. *Frontline.* "How Texas Became a 'Red State.'" KAMU, PBS, April 12, 2005.

Editorial. *Houston Business Journal,* April 3, 1989, 4.

Epps, Garrett. "The Equal Rights Amendment Strikes Again." *Atlantic,* January 20, 2019.

Friedan, Betty. *The Feminine Mystique.* New York: W. W. Norton and Company, 1963.

Hendricks, Judith Jett. "The Office of the Women's Advocate in Houston: An Attempt at Affirmative Action for Women." Master's thesis, University of Houston, 1977.

Houston Breakthrough. Vol. I (June/July 1976); Vol. II (April 1977); "Tribute to Nikki," Vol. III (February 1978).

Houston Chronicle, May 23, 1976; January 4, 1978; July 7, 1987; January 17, 2018.

Houston City, April 1987.

Houston Post, July 8, 1987.

Houston Post archives, March 1974.

Houston Review, vol.1, no. 1.

Jewish Women's Archive. "Bella Abzug." Accessed September 29, 2019. https://jwa.org/womenofvalor/abzug.

——. "Bella Abzug Addresses Fourth World Conference on Women in Beijing." Accessed September 29, 2019. https://jwa.org/thisweek/sep/12/1995/bella-abzug-addresses-world-conference-on-women-in-beijing.

League of Women Voters. "History." Accessed September 29, 2019. https://www.lwv.org/about-us/history.

New York Times, September 5, 2015.

New York Times Archives, April 3, 1977; March 26, 1990.

Nikki Van Hightower Papers, 1967–1997. "Memo to Mayor Hofheinz, July 1, 1977." In Women's Archive and Research Center, Anderson Special Collections, University of Houston Libraries Special Collections.

Playboy Magazine, February 10, 2012.

Ruckelshaus, Jill. "Now Is the Time." 2017. http://www.nowisthetime.org.

Schwab, Nikki. "Ginsburg: Make ERA Part of the Constitution." *U.S. News,* April 18, 2014. Accessed September 29, 2019. https://www.usnews.com/news/blogs/washington-whispers/2014/04/18/justice-ginsburg-make-equal-rights-amendment-part-of-the-constitution.

"Suffragett's Racial Remark Haunts College." *New York Times* Print Archives, May 5, 1996.

Suffragists Oral History Project. Regional Oral History Office, Bancroft Library, University of California, Berkeley.

Texas State Library and Archives Commission, Austin, Texas.

UN Women. "World Conferences on Women." Accessed September 29, 2019. https://www.unwomen.org/en/how-we-work/intergovernmental-support/world-conferences-on-women.

US Department of Education, Office of Civil Rights. "Title IX and Sex Discrimination." Revised April 2015. https://www2.ed.gov/about/offices/list/ocr/docs/tix_dis.html.

Van Hightower, Nikki R. "The Politics of Female Socialization." PhD diss., New York University, October 1974.

——. "What Kind of Women Work at City Hall?" City of Houston employee newsletter. 1977.

Index